y of Congress Cataloging in Publication Data
States. Continental Congress.
ent respect to the opinions of mankind.

des bibliographical references.
nited States—Politics and government—Revolution. 2. United
History—Revolution—Causes. I. Hutson, James H. II. United
ibrary of Congress. American Revolution Bicentennial Office. III.

1975   973.3′1

444-0165-X

sale by the Superintendent of Documents, U.S. Government Printing Office
Washington, D.C. 20402 - Price $5.85
Stock Number 030-001-00063-0

ii

A
Decent Res

to the Opi

of Mank

United States.

CONGRESSIONAL ST

1774–17

Compiled and Edited by
Coordinator, American Revol

LIBRARY OF CONGRESS

Adv
Ame

John
Julia
Lym
Jack
Merr
Cecel
Aubr
Edmu
Richa
    Col
Georg
    sity

Librar
United
A de

Inclu
1. U
States—
States. I
Title.
J10.D74
75-61913
ISBN 0-8

Foreword

THE REVOLUTION may indeed have been "in the minds and hearts of the people," as John Adams wrote many years after it was won, but those leaders taking the fateful steps toward independence made sure, as best they could, that what was in their minds and hearts should be known. The present volume collects and annotates the remarkable series of papers which the Continental Congress issued between 1774 and 1776 to convince British citizens on both sides of the Atlantic that its cause was just. The title of the volume is borrowed, of course, from the first sentence of the Declaration of Independence, a document which was the culmination of Congress' efforts to make its case before the court not only of British but of world opinion.

This volume is but one of several the Library is producing in its Bicentennial program, which has as its theme "Liberty and Learning." A major objective is to make the remarkable richness of the Library's holdings concerning the Revolution better known to the public. We are publishing guides to our Revolutionary-era manuscripts, maps, and graphics, as well as bibliographies of secondary works about the Revolution for adults and young people.

We have been no less concerned, however, to rescue from undeserved obscurity important published primary sources of the Revolutionary era. Thus in 1972 we published *English Defenders of American Freedoms, 1774-1778,* an annotated collection of pamphlets written by British advocates of the American position. Other edited source materials, such as John Paul Jones' memoir to Louis XVI of France, are in preparation and the first two volumes of *Letters of Delegates to Congress, 1774-1789,* a vastly enlarged version of Edmund C. Burnett's earlier work, is in press. But the Library's Bicentennial program ranges all the way from a recorded anthology of American folk music to an exhibition of historic prints and documents entitled "To Set a Country Free" and a series of five scholarly symposia on the Revolution. Thus the Library hopes to illuminate our past and to increase our understanding of the formative period of this nation.

ELIZABETH HAMER KEGAN
Assistant Librarian of Congress

iii

Short Titles of Basic Sources

Burnett, *Letters*
> Edmund C. Burnett, ed., *Letters of Members of the Continental Congress,* 8 vols. (Washington: Carnegie Institution of Washington, 1921–36).

Evans
> Charles Evans, *American Bibliography,* 14 vols. (Chicago: Privately printed for the author by the Blakely Press, 1903–59).

Force, *American Archives*
> Peter Force, ed., *American Archives,* 4th series, 6 vols. (Washington: Published by M. St. Clair Clarke and Peter Force, 1837–46).

JCC
> U.S. Continental Congress, *Journals of the Continental Congress, 1774–1789,* ed. Worthington C. Ford et al., 34 vols. (Washington: Library of Congress, 1904–37).

Contents

iii Foreword

3 Introduction

1774

9 The Association &c.

21 To the People of Great-Britain . . .

33 To the Inhabitants of the Colonies . . .

49 The Bill of Rights [and] a List of Grievances

59 A Letter to the Inhabitants of the Province of Quebec

71 Petition to the King

1775

83 To the Oppressed Inhabitants of Canada

89 A Declaration by the Representatives of the United Colonies . . . Seting Forth the Causes and Necessity of Their Taking up Arms

99 The Twelve United Colonies . . . to the Inhabitants of Great-Britain

109 An Address of the Twelve United Colonies . . . to the People of Ireland

117 Report on Lord North's Conciliatory Proposal

125 The Olive Branch Petition

133 Address to the Assembly of Jamaica

139 A Speech to the Six Confederate Nations . . . From the Twelve United Colonies . . .

1776

149 The Letter to the Inhabitants of the Province of Canada

A DECENT RESPECT

TO THE OPINIONS OF MANKIND

Introduction

COLLECTED HERE are the state papers which the Congress issued before July 4, 1776, to explain the controversy between the American colonies and Great Britain to the world. Congress produced this impressive series of addresses, letters, and petitions for public consumption because it realized that popular opinion was the most potent weapon it could marshal against the fleets and armies of George III. The Members of Congress were among the first leaders of modern times to perceive that political revolution is a struggle for men's minds and that facts and ideas, persuasively and persistently presented, are more effective weapons in that struggle than raw force. In 1774 and 1775 Congress on a number of occasions paid its respects to the opinions of mankind, as Jefferson felicitously put it in the Declaration of Independence. Intellectual altruism may have influenced it somewhat, but self-interest—indeed, self-preservation—was its paramount motive.

The documents included in the present volume were first printed in pamphlets and newspapers that today are accessible in only the largest libraries. Worthington C. Ford reprinted them in his edition of the *Journals of the Continental Congress,* but they are scattered through three volumes and are accompanied by only the barest bibliographical information, which is often misleading. There have been no reprintings since Ford's time.

In addition to the interest which they inspire as revolutionary instrumentalities, these state papers are worth reading because they contain Congress' version of the rise and progress of the controversy with Great Britain and constitute, therefore, the official history of the coming of the American Revolution, a unique chronicle. They are also noteworthy because of their relationship to the Declaration of Independence. It would be absurd to claim that the Declaration cannot be properly understood without reference to them, but its thorough appreciation requires that it be viewed in the context of the state papers whose structure and substance it shares. The Declaration stands in relation to these documents not as an operatic masterpiece to a forgotten overture but as the culminating work in a cycle which throughout reflects a swelling genius. Jefferson himself pronounced the 1774 address to the people of Great Britain "the first composition in the English language," [1] and other of the state papers match it in quality. Documents which illuminate and can stand comparison to the Declaration of Independence merit a reprinting with scholarly apparatus as we mark the 200th anniversaries of the First and Second Continental Congresses.

The arrangement of the papers follows the order in which they were printed rather than that in which Congress adopted them. For example, although the First Continental Congress adopted its petition to the king on October 25 and its letter to the inhabitants of Quebec on October 26, the petition was not published until January 17, 1775, because Congress believed it could not "in point of Decorum be made publick until it has been laid before the Throne." [2] The letter to Quebec thus precedes the petition to the king in this volume.

The printer of the state papers was the Philadelphia partnership of William and Thomas Bradford. One of Philadelphia's early Sons of Liberty, William Bradford was active, with Charles Thomson, John Dickinson, and others, in the Whiggish, antiprerogative politics which coalesced into what opponents in Pennsylvania called, by the late 1760's, the Presbyterian Party.[3] Contrary to some accounts, Bradford was never officially elected Congress' printer,[4] as Thomson, for example, was its secretary. But he was its printer de facto. All state papers were delivered to him for first printing, and newspaper editors and other printers reprinted from him. Employing Bradford as printer was a piece of the same strategy as electing Thomson secretary and choosing Carpenters Hall, rather than the Pennsylvania State House, for the continental meeting place; Congress intended it as a signal that it endorsed the popular cause in Pennsylvania and, by extension, throughout the colonies.

Political credentials aside, Bradford was an excellent printer—some experts consider his *Pennsylvania Journal* technically superior to Franklin's *Pennsylvania Gazette*—who could give Congress what it wanted: quality and speed. The First and Second Congresses were eager to get their proceedings before the public and frequently, as the notes to the documents will show, papers were published within a day or two of their adoption. The Bradfords, for example, produced a volume of the papers of the First Continental Congress one day after that body adjourned. Far from being unusual, therefore, John Dunlap's publication of the broadside of the Declaration of Independence a day after its adoption was consistent with Congress' and the Bradfords' practices during the two preceding years.

There are many other striking similarities between the Declaration of Independence and the state papers of 1774 and 1775. The composition of each was entrusted to a committee, which designated one of its number a draftsman. The draft documents were reported back to the committee for criticism and revision and then went to Congress for additional scrutiny and alteration.

The form of the Declaration of Independence and the state papers (the petitions to the king excepted) is similar. Each begins with a general statement of American rights. A long middle section, detailing the course of the controversy with Great Britain, follows, and a concluding section then declares what action Congress will take to deal with the crisis confronting it.

The Declaration and the state papers are also similar in substance. "There is not an idea in it [the Declaration]," wrote John Adams in 1822, "but what had been hackneyed in Congress for two years before. The substance of it is contained in the declaration of rights and the violation of those rights . . . in 1774." [5] Jefferson, in effect, concurred with Adams' appraisal. In writing the Declaration, he told James Madison in 1823, he had not tried "to find out new principles, or new arguments, never before thought of, not merely to say things which had never been said before; but to place before mankind the common sense of the subject. . . ." The Declaration's authority, he continued, rested "on the harmonizing sentiments of the day." [6]

What sentiments did the Declaration and the state papers share? Most of the British misdeeds, which Jefferson included in his litany of complaints against the king, were identified and deplored in the state papers. The natural rights philosophy, as propounded by John Locke, winds through all the documents. Recent scholars, however, have demoted Locke and his system to a secondary place among the intellectual engines driving the Revolution. Following the lead of Bernard Bailyn, they have given primacy to the ideology of the English opposition writers, which assumed a continual conspiracy of the political high and mighty against liberty. In the Declaration Jefferson noted the putative powerholders' plot in the following terms: "a long train of abuses and usurpations, pursuing inevitably the same Object evinces a design to reduce them [the colonists] under absolute Despotism. . . ." In the state papers the notion of conspiracy is pervasive.

Over and over, Congress complained of a "black and horrid design," [7] formed by the British ministry at the end of the Seven Years' War, to enslave America. And not just America, for Congress believed that the ministry had conceived "a deliberate plan to destroy, in every part of the empire, the free constitution, for which Britain has been so long and so justly famed." [8] Not even the people of England were safe, the delegates believed, for if the ministry subjugated America, it would doubtless turn its instruments of oppression against the mother country. "Soldiers who have sheathed their Swords in the Bowels of their *American* Brethren, will not draw them with more reluctance against you," Congress warned the British people. [9]

It is possible that the notion of conspiracy emerges with particular clarity from the state papers because of the decision of the First Continental Congress not to protest British actions before 1763; compressing the period of American duress into a decade may have invited a simplistic explanation of it. The First

Congress apparently intended to search back to the settlement of the colonies for grievances against Great Britain, but on September 24, 1774, it resolved to confine its attention to the period after 1763.[10] This decision was taken in deference to Virginia. The greater part of Congress, the South Carolina delegates reported, was willing to trace back before 1763 "the many aggressions which had been committed by Great Britain upon her infant Colonies in the jealousies, monopolies, and prohibitions, with which she was so prodigal towards them. . . ." Virginia, the South Carolinians reported, would not "retrospect farther back than to 1763," because it wanted to throw all the odium for America's troubles on George III.[11] Another reason for Virginia's action was offered by Richard Henry Lee, who told John Adams on September 3, 1774, that "to strike against the Navigation Acts would unite every man in Britain against us, because the Kingdom could not exist without them."[12] Lee meant that were Congress to seek to identify grievances inflicted by Britain before 1763, the Navigation Acts would inevitably be attacked and the chances of an accommodation with the mother country would be destroyed.

Congress observed the 1763 restriction in its 1774 and 1775 state papers and Jefferson respected it in writing the Declaration of Independence; he arraigned no British activities before the accession of George III. Although Congress did not officially instruct Jefferson and his fellow committeemen to observe the 1763 limit, there must have been a tacit understanding that they would do so. The idea that America had friends in England worth pleasing was still alive in Congress in July 1776 and, as Jefferson later remarked, forced the deletion of a passage in his draft of the Declaration which "conveyed censures on the people of England."[13] This same idea was evidently strong enough to impose the observation of the 1763 limit on the Declaration itself.

How ironic it is that the draftsman of the document proclaiming the United States free and independent was not himself free to write as he chose but was obliged to observe a restriction designed to conciliate the subjects of the king from whose yoke his countrymen were trying to emancipate themselves. As our approaching Bicentennial focuses renewed attention on the Declaration, this fact should not be forgotten.

***

In compiling these papers I was fortunate in being able to rely upon the assistance of the staff of the Letters of Delegates to Congress project, one of the Library of Congress' American Revolution Bicentennial programs. The editor of the letters, Paul Smith, and his colleagues have allowed me to appropriate to my own use information which they have painstakingly obtained. If there is value in this volume, much of it is owing to them.

NOTES

[1] Stan V. Henkels, ed., "Jefferson's Recollections of Patrick Henry," *Pennsylvania Magazine of History and Biography* 34 (1910):392.

[2] Burnett, *Letters,* 1:84.

[3] For Bradford and the Sons of Liberty, see Frances Cabeen, "The Society of the Sons of Saint Tammany of Philadelphia," *Pennsylvania Magazine of History and Biography* 25 (1901):439; for the Presbyterian Party, see James H. Hutson, *Pennsylvania Politics, 1746–1770* (Princeton: Princeton University Press, 1972), p. 211 ff.

[4] See, for example, John W. Wallace, *An Old Philadelphian, Colonel William Bradford* (Philadelphia: Sherman & Co., printers, 1884), pp. 104, 119–20.

[5] Burnett, *Letters,* 1:516.

[6] Julian P. Boyd, *The Declaration of Independence* (Washington: Library of Congress, 1943), p. 12.

[7] "An Address of the Twelve Colonies . . . to the People of Ireland," p. 111.

[8] "Address to the Assembly of Jamaica," p. 135.

[9] "The Twelve United Colonies . . . to the Inhabitants of Great-Britain," p. 107.

[10] Burnett, *Letters,* 1:53; *JCC,* 1:42.

[11] Burnett, *Letters,* 1:85.

[12] Ibid., 1:3.

[13] Boyd, *Declaration of Independence,* p. 35.

The Association &c.

[Philadelphia: Printed by
William and Thomas Bradford, 1774][1]

Since the American colonies had used commercial coercion in their campaigns to force the British ministry to repeal the Stamp Act and the Townshend Duties, both the delegates to the First Continental Congress and the citizenry at large expected that this weapon would again be employed in the fall of 1774. On September 27 the delegates unanimously agreed that after December 1, 1774, neither British nor Irish goods should be imported and consumed; three days later they resolved that after September 10, 1775, no American merchandise should be exported to Great Britain, Ireland, or the West Indies.[2] On this latter date Congress appointed Thomas Cushing, Isaac Low, Thomas Mifflin, Richard Henry Lee, and Thomas Johnson "a committee to bring in a plan for carrying into effect, the non-importation, non-consumption, and non-exportation resolved on." On October 12 the committee reported what quickly became known as "the plan of Association." It was debated on October 15 and 17 and "after sundry amendments" was adopted on October 18 and ordered to be transcribed for the members' signatures.[3]

Most of the members signed the engrossed copy on October 20, on which day Congress ordered that 120 copies be printed.[4] On October 21 or 22, William and Thomas Bradford delivered the required number of documents, printed on special heavy paper.[5] Then, apparently, the delegates signed each of the 120 copies,[6] so that every colony represented could receive 10 copies authenticated by the signatures of all the delegates.[7] In the meantime, the Bradfords published the Association to the world, printing the signatures of the delegates and appending them to the document.

We do not know the principal draftsman of the Association. A set of rules frequently amended from the floor, it was not one of the more glamorous state papers produced by Congress and rival claimants did not step forward in the years following the Revolution to boast of its paternity. That the Association was the first major document published by the Congress[8] was somewhat peculiar, for it was an instrument for obtaining the redress of American grievances and those grievances, though being formulated, had not yet been announced and were not officially known to the public. But a speedy publication of the Association was mandatory, lest orders for the shipment of British goods, which

*would sabotage nonimportation, be sent to the mother country in real
or feigned ignorance of Congress' intentions. Hence the Association was
rushed into print, with its opening and concluding paragraphs only
briefly explaining the colonies' cause.*

*The significance of the Association is often forgotten. John H. Powell
has correctly described it as "the first act binding on the American
people generally of a constituted American authority larger than, apart
from, the colonial commonwealths. It is the recorded beginnings of the
American government."* [9]

WE, his Majesty's most loyal subjects, the Delegates of the several
Colonies of New-Hampshire, Massachusett's Bay, Rhode-Island,
Connecticut, New-York, New Jersey, Pennsylvania, the Three Lower
Counties of Newcastle, Kent, and Sussex, on Delaware, Maryland, Virginia, North-Carolina, and South-Carolina, deputed to represent them in
a continental Congress, held in the city of Philadelphia, on the fifth day
of September, 1774, avowing our allegiance to his Majesty, our affection
and regard for our fellow-subjects in Great-Britain and elsewhere, affected with the deepest anxiety, and most alarming apprehensions at those
grievances and distresses, with which his Majesty's American subjects are
oppressed, and having taken under our most serious deliberation, the
state of the whole continent, find, that the present unhappy situation
of our affairs, is occasioned by a ruinous system of colony administration
adopted by the British Ministry about the year 1763, evidently calculated
for inslaving these Colonies, and, with them, the British Empire. In
prosecution of which system, various Acts of Parliament have been
passed for raising a Revenue in America, for depriving the American
subjects, in many instances, of the constitutional trial by jury, exposing
their lives to danger, by directing a new and illegal trial beyond the
seas, for crimes alledged to have been committed in America: And in
prosecution of the same system, several late, cruel, and oppressive Acts
have been passed respecting the town of Boston and the Massachusett's-
Bay, and also an Act for extending the province of Quebec, so as to
border on the western frontiers of these Colonies, establishing an
arbitrary government therein, and discouraging the settlement of British
subjects in that wide extended country; thus by the influence of civil

principles and ancient prejudices to dispose the inhabitants to act with hostility against the free protestant Colonies, whenever a wicked Ministry shall chuse so to direct them.

To obtain redress of these grievances, which threaten destruction to the lives, liberty, and property of his Majesty's subjects in North-America, we are of opinion, that a non-importation, non-consumption, and non-exportation agreement, faithfully adhered to, will prove the most speedy, effectual, and peaceable measure: And therefore we do, for ourselves and the inhabitants of the several Colonies, whom we represent, firmly agree and associate under the sacred ties of virtue, honor and love of our country, as follows.

First. THAT from and after the first day of December next, we will not import into British America, from Great Britain or Ireland, any goods, wares or merchandize whatsoever, or from any other place any such goods, wares or merchandize, as shall have been exported from Great-Britain or Ireland; nor will we, after that day, import any East-India tea from any part of the world; nor any molasses, syrrups, paneles, coffee or piemento, from the British plantations, or from Dominica; nor wines from Madeira, or the Western Islands; nor foreign indigo.

Second. THAT we will neither import, nor purchase any slave imported, after the first day of December next; after which time, we will wholly discontinue the slave-trade, and will neither be concerned in it ourselves, nor will we hire our vessels, nor sell our commodities or manufactures to those who are concerned in it.

Third. As a non-consumption agreement, strictly adhered to, will be an effectual security for the observation of the non-importation, we, as above, solemnly agree and associate, that, from this day, we will not purchase or use any Tea imported on account of the East-India company, or any on which a duty hath been or shall be paid; and from and after the first day of March next, we will not purchase or use any East-India tea whatever; nor will we, nor shall any person for or under us, purchase or use any of those goods, wares or merchandize, we have agreed not to import, which we shall know, or have cause to suspect, were imported after the first day of December, except such as come under the rules and directions of the tenth article hereafter mentioned.

Fourth. THE earnest desire we have, not to injure our fellow-subjects in Great Britain, Ireland or the West-Indies, induces us to suspend a non-exportation, until the tenth day of September 1775; at which time, if the said Acts and parts of Acts of the British parliament herein after mentioned are not repealed, we will not, directly or indirectly, export any merchandize or commodity whatsoever to Great Britain, Ireland or the West-Indies, except rice to Europe.

Fifth. Such as are merchants, and use the British and Irish trade, will give orders, as soon as possible, to their factors, agents and correspondents, in Great-Britain and Ireland, not to ship any goods to them, on any pretence whatsoever, as they cannot be received in America; and if any merchant, residing in Great-Britain or Ireland, shall directly or indirectly ship any goods, wares or merchandize, for America, in order to break the said non-importation agreement, or in any manner contravene the same, on such unworthy conduct being well attested, it ought to be made public; and, on the same being so done, we will not from thenceforth have any commercial connexion, with such merchant.

Sixth. That such as are owners of vessels will give positive orders to their captains, or masters, not to receive on board their vessels any goods prohibited by the said non-importation agreement, on pain of immediate dismission from their service.

Seventh. We will use our utmost endeavours to improve the breed of sheep and increase their number to the greatest extent, and to that end, we will kill them as sparingly as may be, especially those of the most profitable kind; nor will we export any to the West-Indies or elsewhere; and those of us who are or may become overstocked with, or can conveniently spare any sheep, will dispose of them to our neighbors, especially to the poorer sort, on moderate terms.

Eighth. That we will in our several stations encourage frugality, oeconomy, and industry; and promote agriculture, arts, and the manufactures of this country, especially that of wool; and will discountenance and discourage, every species of extravagance and dissipation, especially all horse racing, and all kinds of gaming, cock fighting, exhibitions of shews, plays, and other expensive diversions and entertainments. And on the death of any relation or friend, none of us, or any of our families will go into any further mourning dress, than a black crape or ribbon on the arm or hat for Gentlemen, and a black ribbon and necklace for Ladies, and we will discontinue the giving of gloves and scarfs at funerals.

Ninth. THAT such as are venders of goods or merchandize, will not take advantage of the scarcity of goods that may be occasioned by this association, but will sell the same at the rates we have been respectively accuftomed to do, for twelve months last paft.—And if any vender of goods or merchandize, shall sell any such goods on higher terms, or shall in any manner, or by any device whatsoever, violate or depart from this Agreement, no person ought, nor will any of us deal with any such person, or his, or her factor or agent, at any time thereafter, for any commodity whatever.

Tenth. IN case any merchant, trader, or other persons shall import any goods or merchandize after the firft day of December, and before the firft day of February next, the same ought forthwith at the election of the owner, to be either reshipped or delivered up to the Committee of the county, or town wherein they shall be imported, to be ftored at the risque of the importer, until the non-importation Agreement shall cease, or be sold under the direction of the Committee aforesaid; and in the last mentioned case, the owner or owners of such goods, shall be reimbursed (out of the sales) the firft cost and charges, the profit if any, to be applied towards relieving and employing such poor inhabitants of the town of Boston, as are immediate sufferers by the Boston Port-Bill; and a particular account of all goods so returned, ftored, or sold, to be inserted in the public papers; and if any goods or merchandizes shall be imported after the said Firft day of February, the same ought forthwith to be sent back again, without breaking any of the packages thereof.

Eleventh. THAT a Committee be chosen in every county, city, and town, by those who are qualified to vote for Representatives in the Legislature, whose business it shall be attentively to observe the conduct of all persons touching this association; and when it shall be made to appear to the satisfaction of a majority of any such Committee, that any person within the limits of their appointment has violated this association, that such majority do forthwith cause the truth of the case to be published in the Gazette, to the end, that all such foes to the rights of British America may be publickly known, and universally contemned as the enemies of American liberty; and thenceforth we respectively will break off all dealings with him or her.

Twelfth. THAT the Committee of Correspondence in the respective Colonies do frequently inspect the entries of their Custom-Houses, and inform each other from time to time of the true ftate thereof, and of every other material circumſtance that may occur relative to this association.

Thirteenth. THAT all manufactures of this country be sold at reasonable prices, so that no undue advantage be taken of a future scarcity of goods.

Fourteenth. AND we do further agree and resolve, that we will have no trade, commerce, dealings or intercourse whatsoever, with any colony or province, in North-America, which shall not accede to, or which shall hereafter violate this association, but will hold them as unworthy of the rights of freemen, and as inimical to the liberties of their country.

And we do solemnly bind ourselves and our conſtituents, under the ties aforesaid, to adhere to this association until such parts of the several Aćts of Parliament passed since the close of the laſt war, as impose or continue duties on tea, wine, molasses, syrups, paneles, coffee, sugar, piemento, indigo, foreign paper, glass, and painters colours, imported into America, and extend the powers of the Admiralty courts beyond their ancient limits, deprive the American subjećt of trial by jury, author-ise the Judge's certificate to indemnify the proscecutor from damages, that he might otherwise be liable to from a trial by his peers, require oppressive security from a claimant of ships or goods seized, before he shall be allowed to defend his property are repealed [10]—And until that part of the Aćt of the 12. G. 3 ch. 24. entitled, "An Aćt for the better securing his Majeſty's dock yards, magazines, ships, ammunition, and ſtores," by which, any persons charged with committing any of the offences therein described, in America, may be tried in any shire or county within the realm, is repealed [11]—And until the four Aćts passed in the laſt session of Parliament, viz. that for ſtopping the port and blocking up the harbour of Boſton—That for altering charter and government of the Massachusett's-Bay—And that which is entitled, "An Aćt for the better adminiſtration of juſtice, &c." . . . And that "For extending the limits of Quebec, &c." are repealed. And we recommend it to the provincial conventions, and to the committees in the respećtive Colonies, to establish such farther regulations as they may think proper, for carrying into execution this Association.

THE foregoing Association being determined upon by the CONGRESS, was ordered to be subscribed by the several Members thereof; and thereupon we have hereunto set our respećtive names accordingly.

In Congress, Philadelphia, October 20, 1774.

PEYTON RANDOLPH, PRESIDENT.

New Hampshire. { JOHN SULIVAN,
NATHANIEL FOLSOM.

Massachusetts-Bay. { THOMAS CUSHING,
SAMUEL ADAMS,
JOHN ADAMS,
ROBERT TREAT PAINE.

Rhode-Island. { STEPHEN HOPKINS,
SAMUEL WARD.

Connecticut. { ELIPHALET DYER,
ROGER SHERMAN,
SILAS DEANE.

New-York. { ISAAC LOW,
JOHN ALSOP,
JOHN JAY,
JAMES DUANE,
WILLIAM FLOYD,
HENRY WISNER,
S. BOERUM.

New-Jersey. { JAMES KINSEY,
WILLIAM LIVINGSTON,
STEPHEN CRANE,
RICHARD SMITH.

Pensylvania. { JOSEPH GALLOWAY,
JOHN DICKINSON,
CHARLES HUMPHREYS,
THOMAS MIFFLIN,
EDWARD BIDDLE,
JOHN MORTON.

New-Castle, &c. { CÆSAR RODNEY,
THOMAS M'KEAN,
GEORGE READ.

Maryland. { MATTHEW TILGHMAN,
THOMAS JOHNSON,
WILLIAM PACA,
SAMUEL CHASE.

Virginia, { RICHARD HENRY LEE,
GEORGE WASHINGTON,
P. HENRY, Jun.
RICHARD BLAND,
BENJAMIN HARRISON,
EDMUND PENDLETON.

North-Carolina. { WILLIAM HOOPER,
JOSEPH HEWES,
R. CASWELL.

South-Carolina. { HENRY MIDDLETON,
THOMAS LYNCH,
CHRISTOPHER GADSDEN,
JOHN RUTLEDGE,
EDWARD RUTLEDGE.

NOTES

[1] The Library of Congress' copy of the Association was received with the Peter Force documents in 1867. It has no title page but has always been considered, perhaps on the basis of information obtained from Force, to be the first Bradford printing. This attribution is supported by the signatures at the document's end. Note 6, below, documents the fact that the delegates signed the Association on October 20 and at intervals thereafter. George Ross did not sign until October 24. All printings of the Association contain his signature except the first, which was probably produced on October 21 or 22. Since the Library's copy does not contain Ross' signature, it must be the first edition and the traditional attribution appears to be correct.

[2] The South Carolina delegates threatened to refuse to sign the Association unless rice was excepted from nonexportation. They carried their point, over the heated objections

of the delegates from the other colonies and of their colleague Christopher Gadsden. The exception was apparently granted shortly before the Association was signed on October 20. Burnett, *Letters*, 1:85–86.

3 *JCC*, 1:53, 62–63, 75.

4 Ibid., pp. 80–81.

5 Evans, no. 13703.

6Upon receiving Congress' order of October 20 to print 120 copies of the Association, the Bradfords evidently used either the engrossed copy or a fair copy thereof to set in type. They struck off the 120 copies on the special paper and then printed an undetermined number of additional copies on regular paper, printing the signatures from the engrossed copy (this imprint is the text used here). Evans lists as extant three of the 120 copies on special paper: one at the New York Public Library, another at the Historical Society of Pennsylvania, and a third at the Rhode Island Historical Society. The New York Public Library copy bears the signature of New Jersey delegate Richard Smith (indicating his ownership) and the endorsement "Octr. 22d. 1774." In a note at the end of the document, Smith stated: "Patrick Henry Junr. & Edmund Pendleton Esqrs. signed the Original Association but were absent at the signing of this. Messrs. Philip Livingston, John Haring, John D'Hart, Samuel Rhoads, Geo. Ross and Rob. Goldsborough did not sign the Original, being then absent."

Smith's statement that Livingston and others "did not sign the Original" is confirmed by the absence of all their names from the list of the printed signatures on the Association which Bradford printed from the engrossed copy. Yet the engrossed copy, from which Peter Force printed the facsimile in his *American Archives*, 4th series, vol. 1, facing p. 916, and which is now in the National Archives, does in fact contain the signatures of Livingston, De Hart, and Ross. When did they sign? Livingston and De Hart had evidently signed by October 22, for their signatures appear among the other autograph signatures on Richard Smith's copy of the Association, the endorsement on which—October 22—seems to indicate the date of signing. Smith's copy, however, does not contain Ross' signature. Another issue of the Association, bound by Bradford with the *Address to the People of Great Britain* and the *Memorial to the Inhabitants of the British American Colonies* (Evans, no. 13713) and dated October 24, does contain Ross' name among its printed list of signatures. Since Ross took his seat in Congress on the afternoon of October 24, after an absence of some duration (Burnett, *Letters*, 1:82), he apparently signed the Association that afternoon. Thus, like the Declaration of Independence, the Association lay on the table in Congress and was signed at intervals by the members, as they came and went.

7 Later in its life, Congress authenticated documents merely by the signature of its president, its secretary, or both.

8A brief broadside, requesting merchants to refrain from ordering British goods pending the announcement of its actions, was published by order of Congress on September 22, 1774. *JCC*, 1:facing p. 42.

9 John H. Powell, *The Books of a New Nation, United States Government Publications, 1774–1814* (Philadelphia: University of Pennsylvania Press, 1957), p. 38.

10 The Revenue Act of 1764, the "Sugar Act," laid duties on wine, molasses, syrups, paneles (unrefined brown sugar), coffee, sugar, pimiento, and indigo. The Revenue Act of 1766 lowered the duty on molasses. The Townshend Duties of 1767 covered tea, paper, glass, and painters' colors.

The power of the Admiralty Courts, where cases were tried without a jury, was extended by the Sugar Act, which specifically gave them jurisdiction over the Acts of Trade in America and authorized the establishment of a new Admiralty Court. The establishment of additional Vice-Admiralty Courts with original jurisdiction in their districts was authorized by 8 Geo. III, c. 22. The Stamp Act, of course, had prescribed that violators be tried in the Admiralty Courts.

The protection of customs officials from suits for damages by a judge's certificate of probable cause for a seizure and the prevention of an owner's suit for recovery of property unless he first gave security to cover the costs of trial were provisions of the Sugar Act.

11 This statute, the so-called Dockyards Act, declared that any person who set fire to or otherwise destroyed a ship of war, materials, implements, or facilities used to construct the same, or "any of his Majesty's military, naval, or victualling stores or other ammunition of war" was guilty of a felony punishable by death. Offenders who committed the specified crimes in any place out of the realm could be tried for the same "in any shire or county within this realm" at the election of the royal authorities. No specific locality or class of persons was mentioned in the statute, although Congress seemed to assume that the act was directed against America and Americans. The Dockyard Act received the royal assent on April 16, 1772, some weeks before the burning of the *Gaspée* in Rhode Island on June 9, 1772. When news of the incident reached London in July 1772, Lord Hillsborough considered using the act against the arsonists. The law officers of the crown advised him, however, that the act only applied to the destruction of a vessel actually in a dockyard. Merrill Jensen, *The Founding of a Nation* (New York: Oxford University Press, 1968), pp. 426–27; for the text of the Dockyards Act, see Danby Pickering, ed., *The Statutes at Large . . .*, vol. 29 (Cambridge, 1772), pp. 62–63.

To the People of Great-Britain

from the Delegates Appointed by the several ENGLISH COLONIES of NEW-HAMPSHIRE, MASSACHUSETT'S-BAY, RHODE-ISLAND and PROVIDENCE PLANTATIONS, CONNECTICUT, NEW-YORK, NEW-JERSEY, PENNSYLVANIA, The LOWER COUNTIES on DELAWARE, MARYLAND, VIRGINIA, NORTH-CAROLINA, and SOUTH-CAROLINA, to consider of their Grievances in GENERAL CONGRESS, at PHILADELPHIA, September 5th, 1774

Printed from
*Extracts From the Votes and Proceedings of the
American Continental Congress*
(Philadelphia: Printed by
William and Thomas Bradford,
October 27, 1774)

To explain its actions to its two most important audiences, Congress on October 11, 1774, resolved to prepare an address to the people of Great Britain and a memorial to the inhabitants of the colonies. Richard Henry Lee of Virginia, John Jay of New York, and William Livingston of New Jersey were appointed a committee to draft both documents. The committee reported its draft of the address on October 18; it was read and ordered to lie on the table. The next day the address was debated "by paragraphs" and "sundry amendments" were agreed upon. The amendments having been incorporated, the address was approved on October 21 and ordered to be "immediately committed to the press"; as with the Association, no more than 120 copies were to be printed. Congress apparently relaxed this requirement quickly, because on October 24 the Bradfords brought out a large edition of the address, bound with the Association and the memorial to the inhabitants of the colonies. [1]

The claim that John Jay was the author of the address, based on the testimony of Thomas Jefferson in 1805 and on Jay's statement in 1823, [2] *has never been challenged. There is, however, in the Lee Papers at Harvard University a draft address, "To the People of Great Britain and Ireland," in the hand of Jay's fellow committeeman Richard Henry Lee. But aside from one passage which Jay incorporated verbatim (noted below), he seems to have been little influenced by the Lee draft.* [3]

Friends, and Fellow Subjects

WHEN a Nation, led to greatness by the hand of Liberty, and possessed of all the glory that heroism, munificence, and humanity can bestow, descends to the ungrateful task of forging chains for her Friends and Children, and instead of giving support to Freedom, turns advocate for Slavery and Oppression, there is reason to suspect she has either ceased to be virtuous, or been extremely negligent in the appointment of her rulers.

In almost every age, in repeated conflicts, in long and bloody wars, as well civil as foreign, against many and powerful nations, against the open assaults of enemies and the more dangerous treachery of friends, have the inhabitants of your island, your great and glorious ancestors, maintained their independence and transmitted the rights of men and the blessings of liberty to you their posterity.

Be not surprized therefore, that we, who are descended from the same common ancestors; that we, whose forefathers participated in all the rights, the liberties and the constitution, you so justly boast, and who have carefully conveyed the same fair inheritance to us, guarantied by the plighted faith of government and the most solemn compacts with British Sovereigns, should refuse to surrender them to men, who found their claims on no principles of reason, and who prosecute them with a design, that by having our lives and property in their power, they may with the greater facility enslave you.

The cause of America is now the object of universal attention: it has at length become very serious. This unhappy country has not only been oppressed, but abused and misrepresented; and the duty we owe to ourselves and posterity, to your interest, and the general welfare of the British empire, leads us to address you on this very important subject.

Know then, THAT we consider ourselves, and do insist, that we are and ought to be, as free as our Fellow subjects in Britain, and that no power on earth has a right to take our property from us without our consent.

THAT we claim all the benefits secured to the subject by the English constitution, and particularly that inestimable one of trial by jury.

THAT we hold it essential to English Liberty, that no man be condemned unheard, or punished for supposed offences, without having an opportunity of making his defence.

THAT we think the Legislature of Great-Britain is not authorized by the constitution to establish a religion, fraught with sanguinary and impious tenets, or, to erect an arbitrary form of government in any quarter of the globe. These rights, we, as well as you, deem sacred. And yet sacred as they are, they have, with many others, been repeatedly and flagrantly violated.

ARE not the Proprietors of the soil of Great-Britain Lords of their own property? can it be taken from them without their consent? will they yield it to the arbitrary disposal of any man, or number of men whatever?—You know they will not.

WHY then are the Proprietors of the soil of America less Lords of their property than you are of yours, or why should they submit it to the disposal of your Parliament, or any other Parliament, or Council in the world, not of their election? Can the intervention of the sea that divides us, cause disparity in rights, or can any reason be given, why English subjects, who live three thousand miles from the royal palace, should enjoy less liberty than those who are three hundred miles distant from it?

REASON looks with indignation on such distinctions, and freemen can never perceive their propriety. And yet, however chimerical and unjust such discriminations are, the Parliament assert, that they have a right to bind us in all cases without exception, whether we consent or not; that they may take and use our property when and in what manner they please; that we are pensioners on their bounty for all that we possess, and can hold it no longer than they vouchsafe to permit. Such declarations we consider as heresies in English politics, and which can no more operate to deprive us of our property, than the interdicts of the Pope can divest Kings of sceptres which the laws of the land and the voice of the people have placed in their hands.

AT the conclusion of the late war—a war rendered glorious by the abilities and integrity of a Minister,[4] to whose efforts the British empire owes its safety and its fame: At the conclusion of this war, which was succeeded by an inglorious peace, formed under the auspices of a Minister [5] of principles, and of a family unfriendly to the proteſtant cause, and inimical to liberty.—We say at this period, and under the influence of that man, a plan for enslaving your fellow subjeċts in America was concerted, and has ever since been pertinaciously carrying into execution.

PRIOR to this era you were content with drawing from us the wealth produced by our commerce. You reſtrained our trade in every way that could conduce to your emolument. You exercised unbounded sovereignty over the sea. You named the ports and nations to which alone our merchandize should be carried, and with whom alone we should trade; and though some of these reſtrictions were grievous, we nevertheless did not complain; we looked up to you as to our parent ſtate to which we were bound by the strongeſt ties: And were happy in being instrumental to your prosperity and your grandeur.

WE call upon you yourselves, to witness our loyalty and attachment to the common intereſt of the whole empire: Did we not, in the laſt war, add all the strength of this vaſt continent to the force which repelled our common enemy? Did we not leave our native shores, and meet disease and death, to promote the success of British arms in foreign climates? Did you not thank us for our zeal, and even reimburse us large sums of money, which, you confessed, we had advanced beyond our proportion and far beyond our abilities? You did.

To what causes, then, are we to attribute the sudden change of treatment and that system of slavery which was prepared for us at the restoration of peace.

BEFORE we had recovered from the diſtresses which ever attend war, an attempt was made to drain this country of all its money, by the oppressive Stamp-Aċt. Paint, Glass, and other commodities, which you would not permit us to purchase of other nations, were taxed; nay, although no wine is made in any country, subjeċt to the British ſtate, you prohibited our procuring it of foreigners, without paying a tax, imposed by your parliament, on all we imported. These and many other impositions were laid upon us moſt unjuſtly and unconſtitutionally, for the express purpose of raising a Revenue.—In order to silence complaint, it was, indeed, provided, that this revenue should be expended in America for its proteċtion and defence.—These exaċtions, however, can receive no justification from a pretended necessity of protecting and defending us. They are lavishly squandered on court favourites and ministerial dependents, generally avowed enemies to America and employing themselves, by partial representations, to traduce and embroil the Colonies. For the necessary support of government here, we ever were and ever shall be ready to provide. And whenever the exigencies of the state may require it, we shall, as we have heretofore done, chearfully contribute our full proportion of men and money. To enforce this unconstitutional and unjust scheme of taxation, every fence that the wisdom of our British ancestors had carefully erected against arbitrary power, has been violently thrown down in America,[6] and the inestimable right of trial by jury taken away in cases that touch both life and property.—It was ordained, that whenever offences should be committed in the Colonies against particular Acts imposing various duties and restrictions upon trade, the prosecutor might bring his action for the penalties in the Courts of Admiralty; by which means the subject lost the advantage of being tried by an honest uninfluenced jury of the vicinage, and was subjected to the sad necessity of being judged by a single man, a creature of the Crown, and according to the course of a law which exempts the prosecutor from the trouble of proving his accusation, and obliges the defendant either to evince his innocence or to suffer. To give this new indicatory [7] the greater importance, and as, if with design to protect false accusers, it is further provided, that the Judge's certificate of there having been probable causes of seizure and prosecution, shall protect the prosecutor from actions at common law for recovery of damages.

By the course of our law, offences committed in such of the British dominions in which courts are established and justice duely and regularly administred, shall be there tried by a jury of the vicinage. There the offenders and the witnesses are known, and the degree of credibility to be given to their testimony, can be ascertained.

In all these Colonies, justice is regularly and impartially administered, and yet by the construction of some, and the direction of other Acts of Parliament, offenders are to be taken by force, together with all such persons as may be pointed out as witnesses, and carried to England, there to be tried in a distant land, by a *jury* of strangers, and subject to all the disadvantages that result from want of friends, want of witnesses, and want of money.[8]

WHEN the design of raising a revenue from the duties imposed on the importation of tea into America had in great measure been rendered abortive by our ceasing to import that commodity, a scheme was concerted by the Miniftry with the Eaft India Company, and an Act passed enabling and encouraging them to transport and vend it in the Colonies. Aware of the danger of giving success to this insidious manœuvre, and of permitting a precedent of taxation thus to be eftablished among us, various methods were adopted to elude the ftroke. The people of Bofton, then ruled by a Governor, whom, as well as his predecessor Sir Francis Bernard, all America considers as her enemy, were exceedingly embarrassed. The ships which had arrived with the tea were by his management prevented from returning.—The duties would have been paid; the cargoes landed and exposed to sale; a Governor's influence would have procured and protected many purchasers. While the town was suspended by deliberations on this important subject, the tea was destroyed. Even supposing a trespass was thereby committed, and the Proprietors of the tea entitled to damages.—The Courts of Law were open, and Judges appointed by the Crown presided in them.—The Eaft India Company however did not think proper to commence any suits, nor did they even demand satisfaction either from individuals or from the community in general. The Miniftry, it seems, officiously made the case their own, and the great Council of the nation descended to intermeddle with a dispute about private property.—Divers papers, letters, and other unauthenticated ex parte evidence were laid before them; neither the persons who deftroyed the Tea, or the people of Bofton, were called upon to answer the complaint. The Miniftry, incensed by being disappointed in a favourite scheme, were determined to recur from the little arts of finesse, to open force and unmanly violence. The port of Bofton was blocked up by a fleet, and an army placed in the town. Their trade was to be suspended, and thousands reduced to the necessity of gaining subsiftance from charity, till they should submit to pass under the yoke and consent to become slaves, by confessing the omnipotence of Parliament, and acquiescing in whatever disposition they might think proper to make of their lives and property.

LET juftice and humanity cease to be the boaft of your nation! consult your hiftory, examine your records of former transactions, nay turn to the annals of the many arbitrary ftates and kingdoms that surround you, and shew us a single inftance of men being condemned to suffer for imputed crimes, unheard, unqueftioned, and without even the specious formality of a trial; and that too by laws made expressly for the purpose, and which had no exiſtence at the time of the Faᶜt committed. If it be difficult to reconcile these proceedings to the genius and temper of your laws and conſtitution, the task will become more arduous when we call upon our miniſterial enemies to juſtify, not only condemning men untried and by hearsay, but involving the innocent in one common punishment with the guilty, and for the aᶜt of thirty or forty, to bring poverty, diſtress and calamity on thirty thousand souls, and those not your enemies, but your friends, brethren, and fellow subjeᶜts.

It would be some consolation to us, if the catalogue of American oppressions ended here. It gives us pain to be reduced to the necessity of reminding you, that under the confidence reposed in the faith of government, pledged in a royal charter from a British Sovereign, the forefathers of the present inhabitants of the Massachusets-Bay left their former habitations, and eſtablished that great, flourishing, and loyal Colony. Without incurring or being charged with a forfeiture of their rights, without being heard, without being tried, without law, and without justice, by an Act of Parliament, their charter is destroyed, their liberties violated, their conſtitution and form of government changed: And all this upon no better pretence, than because in one of their towns a trespass was committed on some merchandize, said to belong to one of the Companies, and because the Ministry were of opinion, that such high political regulations were necessary to compel due subordination and obedience to their mandates.

Nor are these the only capital grievances under which we labor. We might tell of dissolute, weak and wicked Governors having been set over us; of Legislatures being suspended for asserting the right of British subjects—of needy and ignorant dependents on great men, advanced to the seats of justice and to other places of truſt and importance;—of hard reſtriᶜtions on commerce, and a great variety of lesser evils, the recollection of which is almost lost under the weight and pressure of greater and more poignant calamities.

Now mark the progression of the miniſterial plan for inslaving us.

Well aware that such hardy attempts to take our property from us; to deprive us of that valuable right of trial by jury; to seize our persons, and carry us for trial to Great-Britain; to blockade our ports; to deſtroy our Charters, and change our forms of government, would occasion, and had already occasioned, great discontent in all the Colonies, which might produce opposition to these measures: An Act was passed to protect, indemnify, and screen from punishment such as might be guilty even of murder, in endeavouring to carry their oppressive edicts into execution; And by another Act the dominion of Canada is to be so extended, modelled, and governed, as that by being disunited from us, detached from our interests, by civil as well as religious prejudices, that by their numbers daily swelling with Catholic emigrants from Europe, and by their devotion to Administration, so friendly to their religion, they might become formidable to us, and on occasion, be fit instruments in the hands of power, to reduce the ancient free Protestant Colonies to the same state of slavery with themselves.

THIS was evidently the object of the Act:—And in this view, being extremely dangerous to our liberty and quiet, we cannot forbear complaining of it, as hostile to British America.—Superadded to these considerations, we cannot help deploring the unhappy condition to which it has reduced the many English settlers, who, encouraged by the Royal Proclamation,[9] promising the enjoyment of all their rights, have purchased estates in that country.—They are now the subjects of an arbitrary government, deprived of trial by jury, and when imprisoned cannot claim the benefit of the habeas corpus Act, that great bulwark and palladium of English liberty:—Nor can we suppress our astonishment, that a British Parliament should ever consent to establish in that country a religion that has deluged your island in blood, and dispersed impiety, bigotry, persecution, murder and rebellion through every part of the world.

THIS being a true state of facts, let us beseech you to consider to what end they lead.

ADMIT that the Ministry, by the powers of Britain, and the aid of our Roman Catholic neighbours, should be able to carry the point of taxation, and reduce us to a state of perfect humiliation and slavery. Such an enterprize would doubtless make some addition to your national debt, which already presses down your liberties, and fills you with Pensioners and Placemen——We presume, also, that your commerce will somewhat be diminished. However, suppose you should prove victorious—in what condition will you then be? What advantages or what laurels will you reap from such a conquest?

MAY not a Ministry with the same armies inslave you—it may be said, you will cease to pay them—but remember the taxes from America, the wealth, and we may add, the men, and particularly the Roman Catholics of this vaſt continent will then be in the power of your enemies—nor will you have any reason to expeɕt, that after making slaves of us, many among us should refuse to assiſt in reducing you to the same abjeɕt ſtate.

Do not treat this as chimerical—Know that in less than half a century, the quit rents reserved to the Crown, from the numberless grants of this vaſt continent, will pour large ſtreams of wealth into the royal coffers, and if to this be added the power of taxing America at pleasure, the Crown will be rendered independent on you for supplies, and will possess more treasure than may be necessary to purchase the *remains* of Liberty in your Island.—In a word, take care that you do not fall into the pit that is preparing for us.

WE believe there is yet much virtue, much juſtice, and much public spirit in the English nation—To that juſtice we now appeal. You have been told that we are seditious, impatient of government and desirous of independency. Be assured that these are not faɕts, but calumnies— Permit us to be as free as yourselves, and we shall ever eſteem a union with you to be our greateſt glory and our greateſt happiness, we shall ever be ready to contribute all in our power to the welfare of the Empire—we shall consider your enemies as our enemies, and your intereſt as our own.

BUT if you are determined that your Miniſters shall wantonly sport with the rights of Mankind—If neither the voices of juſtice, the diɕtates of the law, the principles of the conſtitution, or the suggeſtions of humanity can reſtrain your hands from shedding human blood in such an impious cause, we muſt then tell you, that we never will submit to be hewers of wood or drawers of water for any miniſtry or nation in the world.

PLACE us in the same situation that we were at the close of the laſt war, and our former harmony will be reſtored.

BUT leſt the same supineness and the same inattention to our common intereſt, which you have for several years shewn, should continue, we think it prudent to anticipate the consequences.

BY the deſtruction of the trade of Boſton, the Miniſtry have endeavoured to induce submission to their measures.—The like fate may befal us all, we will endeavour therefore to live without trade, and recur for subsistance to the fertility and bounty of our native soil, which will afford us all the necessaries and some of the conveniences of life.—We have suspended our importation from Great Britain and Ireland; and in less than a year's time, unless our grievances should be redressed, shall discontinue our exports to those kingdoms and the West Indies.

It is with the utmost regret however, that we find ourselves compelled by the overruling principles of self-preservation, to adopt measures detrimental in their consequences to numbers of our fellow subjects in Great Britain and Ireland. But we hope, that the magnanimity and justice of the British Nation will furnish a Parliament of such wisdom, independance and public spirit, as may save the violated rights of the whole empire from the devices of wicked Ministers and evil Counsellors whether in or out of office, and thereby restore that harmony, friendship and fraternal affection between all the Inhabitants of his Majesty's kingdoms and territories, so ardently wished for by every true and honest American.

NOTES

[1] *JCC*, 1:62, 75, 81-90, 101. The October 24 printing is in Evans, number 13713.

[2] *Pennsylvania Magazine of History and Biography* 34 (1910):390; Richard H. Lee, *Memoir of the Life of Richard Henry Lee*, vol. 1 (Philadelphia: H.C. Carey and I. Lea, 1825), p. 271.

[3] Lee's draft appears to have evolved from a composition, prepared during the meeting of the Congress, entitled "To the Gentlemen Merchants, and Manufacturers of G. Britain Trading with North America," which is now in the Lee Papers at the University of Virginia. The document was printed in the *Southern Literary Messenger* 30 (March 1860): 173-75.

[4] William Pitt.

[5] John Stuart, 3d Earl of Bute.

[6] This much of the sentence was incorporated verbatim from Richard Henry Lee's draft.

[7] I.e., judicatory.

[8] The Dockyards Act of 1772 authorized the trial in Britain of alleged perpetrators of crimes in America, as did the Administration of Justice Act, May 20, 1774, one of the

"Intolerable Acts," which declared that if a magistrate or customs official, or others acting under their authority, were indicted for murder in Massachusetts, the governor, if he judged a fair trial to be impossible in the colonies, could order the defendant brought to Britain for trial. In December 1768 the House of Lords and in February 1769 the House of Commons passed resolutions encouraging the king to use 35 Henry VIII, c. 2, which authorized trials in England for treason or misprision of treason, committed outside of the realm, against malefactors in Massachusetts. The royal commission of inquiry, established in August 1772 to investigate the burning of the *Gaspée*, was empowered to use 35 Henry VIII, c. 2, against Americans. For the Henry VIII statute, which excited considerable comment in the Continental Congress, see Lawrence H. Gipson, *The British Empire Before the American Revolution*, 15 vols. (Caldwell, Idaho: Caxton Printers; New York: Alfred A. Knopf, 1936-70). 11:254-58, and William R. Leslie, "The Gaspée Affair: A Study of Its Constitutional Significance," *Mississippi Valley Historical Review* 39 (September 1952): 239-46.

[9] The Proclamation of 1763 pledged that settlers in Quebec and the other new provinces should enjoy representative assemblies "in such manner and form as is used and directed in those colonies and provinces in America, which are under our immediate government"; furthermore, the king declared that "all persons inhabiting in, or resorting to, our said colonies, may confide in our royal protection for the enjoyment of the benefit of the laws of our realm of England." Merrill Jensen, ed., *English Historical Documents*, vol. 9 (London: Eyre & Spottiswoode, 1955), pp. 640-43.

To the Inhabitants of the Colonies

of New-Hampshire, Massachusetts-Bay, Rhode-Island and Providence Plantations; Connecticut, New-York, New-Jersey, Pennsylvania, the Counties of Newcastle, Kent and Sussex on Delaware; Maryland, Virginia, North Carolina and South Carolina.

Printed from
Extracts From the Votes and Proceedings of the American Continental Congress
(Philadelphia: Printed by
William and Thomas Bradford,
October 27, 1774)

The committee, consisting of Richard Henry Lee, John Jay, and William Livingston, which had reported the address to the people of Great Britain on October 18, reported a draft of the memorial to the inhabitants of the colonies on October 19. The memorial was debated on October 20 and 21 and approved and sent to the printer on the latter date. The Bradfords published it at the same time and in the same manner as they did the address.[1]

Authorship of the memorial has always been ascribed to Richard Henry Lee.[2] Yet when the R. R. Logan Collection at the Historical Society of Pennsylvania was opened to scholars in 1969, it yielded a 17-page draft of the memorial in John Dickinson's hand, which was indisputably the text of the document adopted by Congress.

The genesis of the Dickinson draft is a mystery and will probably remain one, because no information survives about the composition of the memorial. Dickinson did not take his seat in Congress until October 17 [3] and he was not, of course, a member of the committee appointed to draft the memorial. But since his reputation as a penman was so formidable, since his authority with the delegates was so great, and since he may have been privy to what was occurring in Congress before taking his seat,[4] it is conceivable that the committee appointed on October 11 to draft the memorial appealed to him to produce this important state paper. On the other hand, Dickinson may have been pressed into service on October 19 by a Congress disappointed with the handiwork of its committee. Whatever the case, the newly discovered draft in the Logan Papers establishes a major role for Dickinson in the composition of the memorial.

FRIENDS AND FELLOW COUNTRYMEN,

W E, the Delegates appointed by the good people of the above Colonies to meet at Philadelphia in September laſt, for the purposes mentioned by our reſpective Conſtituents, have in pursuance of the truſt reposed in us, assembled, and taken into our moſt serious consideration the important matters recommended to the Congress. Our resolutions thereupon will be herewith communicated to you. But as the situation of public affairs grows daily more and more alarming; and as it may be more satisfactory to you to be informed by us in a collective body, than in any other manner, of those sentiments that have been approved, upon a full and free discussion by the Representatives of so great a part of America, we eſteem ourselves obliged to add this Address to these Resolutions.

IN every case of opposition by a people to their rulers, or of one ſtate to another, duty to Almighty God, the creator of all, requires that a true and impartial judgment be formed of the measures leading to such opposition; and of the causes by which it has been provoked, or can in any degree be juſtified: That neither affeſtion on the one hand, nor resentment on the other, being permitted to give a wrong bias to reason, it may be enabled to take a dispassionate view of all the circumſtances, and settle the public conduſt on the solid foundations of wisdom and juſtice.

FROM Councils thus tempered arise the sureſt hopes of the divine favour, the firmeſt encouragement to the parties engaged and the strongeſt recommendation of their cause to the reſt of mankind.

WITH minds deeply impressed by a sense of these truths, we have diligently, deliberately and calmly enquired into and considered those exertions, both of the legislative and executive power of Great-Britain, which have excited so much uneasiness in America, and have with equal fidelity and attention considered the conduſt of the Colonies. Upon the whole, we find ourselves reduced to the disagreeable alternative, of being silent and betraying the innocent, or of speaking out and censuring those we wish to revere.—In making our choice of these diſtressing difficulties, we prefer the course dictated by honesty, and a regard for the welfare of our country.

Soon after the conclusion of the late war, there commenced a memorable change in the treatment of these Colonies. By a statute made in the fourth year of the present reign, a time of *profound peace,* alledging "the expediency of new provisions and regulations for extending the commerce between Great-Britain and his Majesty's dominions in America, and the *necessity* of *raising a Revenue* in the said dominions for defraying the expences of *defending,* protecting and securing the same," the *Commons of Great-Britain* undertook to *give* and *grant* to his Majesty many rates and duties, to be paid in these Colonies. To enforce the observance of this Act, it prescribes a great number of severe penalties and forfeitures; and in two sections makes a remarkable distinction between the subjects in Great-Britain and those in America. By the one, the penalties and forfeitures incurred *there* are to be recovered in any of the King's Courts of *Record* at *Westminster,* or in the Court of Exchequer in Scotland; and by the other, the penalties and forfeitures incurred *here* are to be recovered in any Court of Record, or in any Court of *Admiralty* or *Vice-Admiralty, at the election of the informer or prosecutor.*

The Inhabitants of these Colonies confiding in the justice of Great-Britain, were scarcely allowed sufficient time to receive and consider this Act, before another, well known by the name of the *Stamp Act,* and passed in the fifth year of this reign, engrossed their whole attention. By this statute the British Parliament exercised in the most explicit manner a power of *taxing* us, and extending the jurisdiction of Courts of *Admiralty* and *Vice-Admiralty* in the Colonies, to matters arising within the body of a county, directed the numerous penalties and forfeitures, thereby inflicted, to be recovered in the said Courts.

In the same year a tax was imposed upon us, by an Act establishing several new fees in the customs.[5] In the next year, the Stamp Act was repealed; not because it was founded in an erroneous principle, but, as the repealing Act recites, because "the continuance thereof would be attended with many inconveniences, and might be productive of consequences greatly detrimental to the commercial interest of Great-Britain."

In the same year, and by a subsequent Act, it was declared, "that his Majesty in Parliament, of right, had power to bind the people of these

36

Colonies by Statutes IN ALL CASES WHATSOEVER."

IN the same year, another Act was passed, for imposing rates and duties payable in these Colonies. In this Statute the Commons avoiding the terms of *giving* and *granting* "humbly besought his Majesty that it might be enacted &c." But from a declaration in the preamble, that the rates and duties were "in lieu of" several others granted by the Statute first before mentioned *for raising a revenue* and from some other expressions it appears, that these duties were intended *for that purpose.*

IN the next year (1767), an Act was made "to enable his Majesty to put the customs and *other duties* in America under the management of Commissioners &c." and the King thereupon erected the present expensive Board of Commissioners, for the express purpose of carrying into execution the several Acts relating to the *revenue* and trade in *America.*

AFTER the repeal of the Stamp-Act, having again resigned ourselves to our antient unsuspicious affections for the parent state, and anxious to avoid any controversy with her, in hopes of a favourable alteration in sentiments and measures towards us, we did not press our objections against the above mentioned Statutes made subsequent to that repeal.

ADMINISTRATION attributing to trifling causes, a conduct that really proceeded from generous motives, were encouraged in the same year (1767) to make a bolder experiment on the patience of America.

BY a Statute commonly called the *Glass, Paper and Tea Act,* made fifteen months after the repeal of the *Stamp-Act,* the Commons of Great-Britain resumed their former language, and again undertook to *"give* and *grant* rates and duties to be paid in these Colonies," for the express purpose of *"raising a revenue,* to defray the charges of the *administration of justice,* the support of *civil government,* and *defending* the Kings dominions," on this continent. The penalties and forfeitures, incurred under this Statute, are to be recovered *in the same manner,* with those mentioned in the foregoing Acts.

TO this Statute, so naturally tending to disturb the tranquillity then universal throughout the Colonies, Parliament, in the same session, added another no less extraordinary.

EVER since the making the present peace, a standing army has been

37

kept in these Colonies. From respect for the mother country, the inno-vation was not only tolerated, but the provincial Legislatures generally made provision for supplying the troops.

THE Assembly of the province of New York, having passed an Act of this kind, but differing in some articles, from the directions of the Act of Parliament made in the *fifth* year of this reign, the House of Representatives in that Colony was prohibited by a Statute made in the session last mentioned, from making any bill, order, resolution or vote, except for adjourning or chusing a Speaker, until provision should be made by the said Assembly for furnishing the troops within that prov-ince, not only with all such necessaries as were required by the Statute *which they were charged with disobeying,* but also with those required by two other *subsequent* Statutes, which were declared to be in force until the twenty fourth day of March 1769.

THESE Statutes of the year 1767 revived the apprehensions and dis-contents, that had entirely subsided on the repeal of the *Stamp-Act;* and amidst the just fears and jealousies thereby occasioned, a Statute was made in the next year (1768) to establish Courts of *Admiralty* and *Vice Admiralty* on a new model, expressly for the end of more *effectually* recovering the *penalties* and *forfeitures* inflicted by Acts of Parliament, framed for the purpose of *raising a revenue* in America, &c.

THE immediate tendency of these statutes is, to subvert the right of having a share in legislation, by rendering Assemblies useless; the right of property, by taking the money of the Colonists without their consent; the right of trials by jury, by substituting in their place trials in Ad-miralty and Vice-Admiralty Courts, where single Judges preside, hold-ing their Commissions during pleasure; and unduly to influence the Courts of common law, by rendering the Judges thereof totally depen-dent on the Crown for their salaries.

THESE statutes, not to mention many others exceedingly exceptionable, compared one with another, will be found, not only to form a regular system, in which every part has great force, but also a pertinacious ad-herence to that system, for subjugating these Colonies, that are not, and from local circumstances, cannot be represented in the House of Com-mons, to the uncontroulable and unlimited power of Parliament, in violation of their undoubted rights and liberties, in contempt of their humble and repeated supplications.

THIS conduct must appear equally astonishing and unjustifiable, when it is considered how unprovoked it has been by any behaviour of these Colonies. From their first settlement, their bitterest enemies never fixed on any of them a charge of disloyalty to their Sovereign or disaffection to their Mother-Country. In the wars she has carried on, they have exerted themselves whenever required, in giving her assistance; and have rendered her services, which she has publickly acknowledged to be extremely important. Their fidelity, duty and usefulness during the last war, were frequently and affectionately confessed by his late Majesty and the present King.

THE reproaches of those, who are most unfriendly to the freedom of America, are principally levelled against the province of Massachusetts-Bay; but with what little reason, will appear by the following declarations of a person, the truth of whose evidence, in their favour, will not be questioned—Governor Bernard thus addresses the two Houses of Assembly—in his speech on the 24th of April 1762,—"The unanimity and dispatch, with which you have complied with the *requisitions of his Majesty,* require my particular acknowledgement. And it gives me additional pleasure to observe, that you have therein acted under no other influence than a due sense of your duty, both as members of a general empire, and as the body of a particular province."

IN another speech on the 27th of May, in the same year, he says,— "Whatever shall be the event of the war, it must be no small satisfaction to us, that this province hath contributed its full share to the support of it. *Every thing that hath been required of it hath been complied with;* and the execution of the powers committed to me, for raising the provincial troops hath been as full and complete as the grant of them. Never before were regiments so easily levied, so well composed, and so early in the field as they have been this year; the common people seemed to be animated with the spirit of the general Court, and to vie with them in their readiness to serve the King."

SUCH was the conduct of the People of the Massachusetts-Bay, during the last war. As to their behaviour before that period, it ought not to have been forgot in Great-Britain, that not only on every occasion they had constantly and chearfully complied with the frequent royal requisitions—but that chiefly by their vigorous efforts, Nova-Scotia was subdued in 1710, and Louisbourg in 1745.

FOREIGN quarrels being ended, and the domestic disturbances, that quickly succeeded on account of the stamp-act, being quieted by its repeal, the Assembly of Massachusetts-Bay transmitted an humble address of thanks to the King and divers Noblemen, and soon after passed a bill for granting compensation to the sufferers in the disorder occasioned by that act.

THESE circumstances and the following extracts from Governor Bernard's Letters in 1768, to the Earl of Shelburne, Secretary of State,[6] clearly shew, with what grateful tenderness they strove to bury in oblivion the unhappy occasion of the late discords, and with what respectful reluctance they endeavoured to escape other subjects of future controversy. "The House, (says the Governor) from the time of opening the session to this day, has shewn a disposition to *avoid* all dispute with me; every thing having passed with as much good humour as I could desire, except only their continuing to act in *addressing* the King, *remonstrating* to the Secretary of State, and *employing* a separate agent. It is the *importance of this innovation,* without any wilfulness of my own, which induces me to make this remonstrance at a time when I have a fair prospect of having, *in all other business,* nothing but good to say of the proceedings of the House." *

"THEY have acted *in all things,* even in their remonstrance *with temper and moderation;* they have *avoided* some subjects of dispute, and have laid a foundation for *removing* some causes of former altercation." †

"I shall make such a prudent and proper use of this Letter as, I hope, will perfectly restore the peace and tranquillity of this province, for which purpose *considerable steps have been made by the House of Representatives.*"**

THE vindication of the province of Massachusetts-Bay contained in these Letters will have greater force, if it be considered, that they were written several months after the fresh alarm given to the colonies by the statutes passed in the preceding year.

IN this place it seems proper to take notice of the insinuation in one of these statutes, that the interference of Parliament was *necessary* to provide for "defraying the charge of the *administration of justice,* the sup-

*January 21, 1768.   †January 30, 1768.   **February 2, 1768.

port of *civil government,* and defending the King's dominions in America."

As to the two firſt articles of expence, every colony had made such provision, as by their respeċtive Assemblies, the best judges on such occasions, was thought expedient, and suitable to their several circumſtances. Respeċting the laſt, it is well known to all men the leaſt acquainted with American affairs, that the colonies were eſtablished, and have generally defended themselves, without the leaſt assiſtance from Great-Britain; and, that at the same time her *taxing* them by the ſtatutes before mentioned, moſt of them were labouring under very heavy debts contraċted in the laſt war. So far were they from sparing their money, when their Sovereign, conſtitutionally, asked their aids, that during the course of that war, Parliament repeatedly made them compensations for the expences of those ſtrenuous efforts, which, consulting their zeal rather than their ſtrength, they had chearfully incurred.

SEVERE as the Aċts of *Parliament* before-mentioned are, yet the conduċt of *Adminiſtration* has been equally injurious, and irritating to this devoted country.

UNDER pretence of governing them, so many new inſtitutions, uniformly rigid and dangerous, have been introduced, as could only be expeċted from incensed maſters, for collecting the tribute or rather the plunder of conquered provinces.

BY an order of the King, the authority of the Commander in chief, and under him of the Brigadiers general, *in time of peace,* is rendered *supreme* in all the civil governments in *America;* and thus an uncontroulable military power is veſted in officers not known to the conſtitution of these colonies.

A LARGE body of troops and a considerable armament of ships of war have been sent to assiſt in taking their money without their consent.

EXPENSIVE and oppressive offices have been multiplied, and the aċts of corruption induſtriously praċtised to divide and deſtroy.

THE Judges of the Admiralty and Vice Admiralty Courts are impowered to receive their salaries and fees from the effeċts to be condemned by themselves; the Commissioners of the cuſtoms are impowered to break open and enter houses without the authority of any civil magistrate founded on legal information.

JUDGES of Courts of Common Law have been made entirely dependent on the Crown for their commissions and salaries.

A COURT has been established at Rhode-Island, for the purpose of taking Colonists to England to be tried.

HUMBLE and reasonable petitions from the Representatives of the people have been frequently treated with contempt; and Assemblies have been repeatedly and arbitrarily dissolved.

FROM some few instances it will sufficiently appear, on what pretences of justice those dissolutions have been founded.

THE tranquility of the colonies having been again disturbed, as has been mentioned, by the statutes of the year 1767, the Earl of Hillsborough, Secretary of State, in a letter to Governor Bernard, dated April 22, 1768, censures the *"presumption"* of the House of Representatives for "resolving upon a measure of so inflammatory a nature *as that of writing to the other colonies, on the subject of their intended representations against some late Acts of Parliament,"* then declares that, "his Majesty considers this step as evidently tending to create unwarrantable combinations to excite an unjustifiable opposition to the constitutional authority of Parliament."—and afterwards adds,—It is *the King's pleasure,* that as soon as the General Court is again assembled, at the time prescribed by the Charter, you should require of the House of Representatives, in his Majesty's name, to *rescind* the resolution which gave birth to the circular letter from the Speaker, and to declare their disapprobation of, and dissent to that rash and hasty proceeding."

"If the new Assembly should refuse to comply with his Majesty's reasonable expectation, it is the King's pleasure, that you should immediately dissolve them."

This letter being laid before the House, and the resolution not being rescinded according to the order, the Assembly was dissolved. A letter of a similar nature was sent to other Governors to procure resolutions approving the conduct of the Representatives of Massachusetts-Bay, to be *rescinded* also; and the Houses of Representatives in other colonies refusing to comply, Assemblies were dissolved.

THESE mandates spoke a language, to which the ears of English subjects had for several generations been strangers. The nature of assemblies implies a power and right of deliberation; but these commands, proscribing the exercise of judgment on the propriety of the requisitions made, left to the Assemblies only the election between dictated submission and the threatened punishment: A punishment too, founded on no other act, than such as is deemed innocent even in slaves—of agreeing in *petitions* for redress of grievances, that equally affected all.

THE hostile and unjustifiable invasion of the town of Boston soon followed these events in the same year; though that town, the province in which it is situated, and all the colonies, from abhorrence of a contest with their parent state, permitted the execution even of those statutes, against which they so unanimously were complaining, remonstrating and supplicating.

ADMINISTRATION, determined to subdue a spirit of freedom, which English Ministers should have *rejoiced* to cherish, entered into a monopolising combination with the East-India company, to send to this continent vast quantities of Tea, an article on which a duty was laid by a statute, that, in a particular manner, attacked the liberties of America, and which therefore the inhabitants of these Colonies had resolved not to import. The cargo sent to South-Carolina was stored, and not allowed to be sold. Those sent to Philadelphia and New-York were not permitted to be landed. That sent to Boston was destroyed, because Governor Hutchinson would not suffer it to be returned.

ON the intelligence of these transactions arriving in Great-Britain, the public spirited town last mentioned was singled out for destruction, and it was determined, the province it belongs to should partake of its fate. In the last session of parliament therefore were passed the acts for shutting up the port of Boston, indemnifying the murderers of the inhabitants of Massachusetts-Bay, and changing their chartered constitution of government. To inforce these acts, that province is again invaded by a fleet and army.

To mention these outrageous proceedings, is sufficient to explain them. For tho' it is pretended, that the province of Massachusetts-Bay has been particularly disrespectful to Great-Britain, yet in truth the behaviour of

43

the people, in other colonies, has been an equal "opposition to the power assumed by "parliament." No ſtep however has been taken againſt any of the reſt. This artful conduct conceals several designs. It is expected that the province of Massachusetts-Bay will be irritated into some violent action, that may displease the reſt of the continent, or that may induce the people of Great-Britain to approve the meditated vengeance of an imprudent and exasperated miniſtry.

IF the unexampled pacifick temper of that province shall disappoint this part of the plan, it is hoped the other colonies will be so far intimidated as to desert their brethren, suffering in a common cause, and that thus disunited all may be subdued.

To promote these designs, another measure has been pursued. In the session of parliament laſt mentioned, an act was passed, for changing the government of Quebec, by which act the Roman Catholic religion, instead of being tolerated, as ſtipulated by the treaty of peace, is eſtablished; and the people there deprived of the right to an assembly, trials by jury and the English laws in civil cases abolished, and inſtead thereof, the French laws eſtablished, in direct violation of his Majeſty's promise by his royal proclamation, under the faith of which many English subjects settled in that province: and the limits of that province are extended so as to comprehend those vaſt regions, that lie adjoining to the northernly and weſternly boundaries of these colonies.

THE authors of this arbitrary arrangement flatter themselves, that the inhabitants, deprived of liberty, and artfully provoked againſt those of another religion, will be proper inſtruments for assiſting in the oppression of such, as differ from them in modes of government and faith.

FROM the detail of facts herein before recited, as well as from authentic intelligence received, it is clear beyond a doubt, that a resolution is formed and now is carrying into execution, to extinguish the freedom of these colonies, by subjecting them to a despotic government.

AT this unhappy period, we have been authorized and directed to meet and consult together for the welfare of our common country. We accepted the important truſt with diffidence, but have endeavoured to discharge it with integrity. Though the ſtate of these colonies would certainly juſtify other measures than we have advised, yet weighty reasons determined us to prefer those which we have adopted. In the firſt place, it appeared to us a conduct becoming the character, these colonies have ever sustained, to perform, even in the midst of the unnatural distresses and imminent dangers that surround them, every act of loyalty; and therefore, we were induced to offer once more to his Majesty the petitions of his faithful and oppressed subjects in America. Secondly, regarding with the tender affection, which we knew to be so universal among our countrymen, the people of the kingdom, from which we derive our original, we could not forbear to regulate our steps by an expectation of receiving full conviction, that the colonists are equally dear to them. Between these provinces and that body, subsists the social band, which we ardently wish *may never* be dissolved, and which *cannot* be dissolved, until their minds shall become *indisputably hostile,* or their *inattention* shall permit those who are thus hostile to persist in prosecuting with the powers of the realm the destructive measures already operating against the colonists; and in either case, shall reduce the latter to such a situation, that they shall be compelled to renounce every regard, but that of self-preservation. Notwithstanding the vehemence with which affairs have been impelled, they have not yet reached that fatal point. We do not incline to accelerate their motion, already alarmingly rapid; we have chosen a method of opposition, that does not preclude a hearty reconciliation with our fellow-citizens on the other side of the Atlantic. We deeply deplore the urgent necessity that presses us to an immediate interruption of commerce, that may prove injurious to them. We trust they will acquit us of any unkind intentions towards them, by reflecting, that we subject ourselves to similar inconveniences; that we are driven by the hands of violence into unexperienced and unexpected public convulsions, and that we are contending for freedom, so often contended for by our ancestors.

THE people of England will soon have an opportunity of declaring their sentiments concerning our cause.[7] In their piety, generosity, and good sense, we repose high confidence; and cannot, upon a review of past events, be persuaded, that *they,* the defenders of true religion, and the assertors of the rights of mankind, will take part against their affectionate protestant brethren in the colonies, in favour of *our open* and *their own secret* enemies, whose intrigues, for several years past, have been wholly exercised in sapping the foundations of civil and religious liberty.

ANOTHER reason, that engaged us to prefer the commercial mode of

45

opposition, arose from an assurance, that this mode will prove efficacious, if it be persisted in with fidelity and virtue; and that your conduct will be influenced by these laudable principles, cannot be questioned. Your own salvation, and that of your posterity, now depends upon yourselves. You have already shewn that you entertain a proper sense of the blessings you are striving to retain. Against the temporary inconveniences you may suffer from a stoppage of trade, you will weigh in the opposite balance, the endless miseries you and your descendants must endure from an established arbitrary power. You will not forget the honour of your country, that must from your behaviour take its title in the estimation of the world, to glory, or to shame; and you will, with the deepest attention, reflect, that if the peaceable mode of opposition recommended by us, be broken and rendered ineffectual, as your cruel and haughty ministerial enemies, from a contemptuous opinion of your firmness, insolently predict will be the case, you must inevitably be reduced to chuse, either a more dangerous contest, or a final, ruinous, and infamous submission.

MOTIVES thus cogent, arising from the emergency of your unhappy condition, must excite your utmost diligence and zeal, to give all possible strength and energy to the pacific measures calculated for your relief: But we think ourselves bound in duty to observe to you, that the schemes agitated against these colonies have been so conducted, as to render it prudent, that you should extend your views to the most unhappy events, and be in all respects prepared for every contingency. Above all things we earnestly intreat you, with devotion of spirit, penitence of heart, and amendment of life, to humble yourselves, and implore the favour of almighty God: and we fervently beseech his divine goodness, to take you into his gracious protection.

NOTES

1 *JCC*, 1:62, 75, 81, 90-101.

2 On the basis, principally, of Jay's statement to Lee's grandson in 1823: "On the 18th October, the *address* to the people of Great Britain was reported to Congress. . . . On the 19th October, the committee reported a draught of a *memorial* to the inhabitants of the British colonies. . . . I have always believed that this memorial was written by Mr. Lee,

nor have any reasons to doubt it, come to my knowledge." Richard H. Lee, *Memoir of the Life of Richard Henry Lee,* vol. 1 (Philadelphia: H. C. Carey and I. Lea, 1825), p. 271.

[3] *JCC,* 1:74.

[4] See the discussion of Dickinson's role in the preparation of the Bill of Rights, below.

[5] 5 Geo. III, c. 45, "An act for more effectually securing and encouraging the trade of his Majesty's American dominions . . . and for regulating the fees of the officers of the customs in the said dominions."

[6] Letters written in 1768 by Bernard and by the military commanders and customs commissioners in Boston were obtained in England by William Bollan and sent to the popular leaders in Massachusetts, who published them in the *Boston Gazette* in 1769. That Samuel Adams wrote an extended commentary on them in a pamphlet, *An Appeal to the World; Or, a Vindication of the Town of Boston* . . . (Boston, 1769), leads to the assumption that he supplied the Bernard material to the author of this memorial. See Francis G. Walett, "Governor Bernard's Undoing: An Earlier Hutchinson Letters Affair," *New England Quarterly* 38 (1965): 217-26.

[7] The Septennial Act of 1715 required that parliamentary elections be held every seven years. Parliament had been sitting since 1768 and the Americans expected general elections in the spring of 1775, time enough for the measures adopted by the Continental Congress to have an impact on the British electorate. Lord North, however, dissolved Parliament and called for new elections on September 30, 1774. The suspicions of American leaders that his action was dictated by fear of the Continental Congress were unfounded, because North had resolved to dissolve Parliament as early as July 6, 1774. Lewis Namier and John Brooke, *The House of Commons, 1754-1790* (New York: Oxford University Press, 1964), pp. 73-74, 535.

The Bill of Rights
[and]
a List of Grievances

Printed from
*Extracts From the Votes and Proceedings of the
American Continental Congress*
(Philadelphia: Printed by
William and Thomas Bradford,
October 27, 1774)

It is no easier to establish authorship of the declaration of rights and grievances than it is of the Association, because both documents were products of constant debate on the floor of Congress. The delegates clearly conceived of the codification of colonial rights as their principal duty. Most, evidently, considered themselves heirs of the English patriots who, during the Glorious Revolution a century earlier, had deliberated and produced the Bill of Rights, one of the wonders of the English-speaking world. Congress, in fact, soon slipped into the habit of referring to its statement of rights as a Bill of Rights.

On September 7, 1774, Congress appointed two members from each colony to a committee to formulate rights and grievances. According to John Adams' autobiography, this "grand Committee" appointed a subcommittee which prepared a draft and reported it back to the full committee, where it was vigorously debated.[1] The committee submitted to Congress "a report of the Rights" on September 22 and "a report of the infringements and violations" thereof on September 24.

These reports were evidently not actively considered until October 12. Then, they were debated until October 14, when tentative agreement was apparently reached on them.[2] Samuel Ward's diary and James Duane's notes indicate, however, that grievances were being discussed, in some manner, as late as October 17.[3] Although the Journals of Congress are silent on the matter, Duane noted that on October 14 a committee was appointed "to state in form the Rights, Grievances, and mode of redress."[4] In his autobiography, John Adams recalled that he "was appointed to put them into form and report a fair Draught for their final Acceptance," a statement which appears to be confirmed by an entry in his diary for Sunday, October 16, 1774: "staid at home all day; very busy in the necessary business of putting the proceedings of the Congress into order."[5] We do not know when a fair copy finally issued from the committee of which Adams was a member or when Congress approved it. That Secretary Thomson entered the official version of the Bill of Rights in the Journals under the date of October 14 shows that in this instance, as in others, he was not as meticulous as he might have been.

Two mysteries attend the Bill of Rights. One is the so-called "Sullivan's Draught" of the document. In his autobiography John Adams *stated that New Hampshire delegate John Sullivan had prepared "a sett of Articles" listing the colonies' grievances.[6] In editing his grandfather's papers, Charles Francis Adams discovered an early draft of the Bill of Rights in a hand "somewhat resembling that of Major Sullivan," which he printed in the appendix in parallel columns with the official Bill of Rights.[7] In editing the* Journals of Congress, *Worthington C. Ford followed Adams' lead and printed the two versions of the document in parallel columns, labeling the earlier one "Sullivan's Draught."[8] The editors of the current, definitive edition of Adams' papers have rejected Ford's attribution; "the paper is not in Sullivan's hand," they declare, "though neither has the hand so far been identified as that of any other member of the committee on rights. . . ."[9] By careful collation the editors of the forthcoming* Letters of Delegates to Congress, 1774–1789, *one of the Library of Congress' American Revolution Bicentennial projects, have established that the draft is in the hand of John Dickinson.*

That Adams, as a member of a committee to prepare a final version of the Bill of Rights, should have had in his possession an earlier draft of the document is not unusual. What is surprising is that the draft should have been written by Dickinson, who did not take his seat in Congress until October 17. Dickinson, while still a private citizen, may thus have been not only privy to Congress' business but even entrusted with the drafting of important documents. Congress may have been eager to employ the talents of the most famous political pamphleteer in America, who thereby would have become the national government's first consultant.

On the other hand, Dickinson may not have written his draft until after he took his seat in Congress. This would mean that as of October 17 Congress still had not decided upon the final form of the Bill of Rights and List of Grievances. Such an assumption would help solve the other mystery attending the Bill of Rights: why was it not published until October 27, 1774, in the Extracts from the Votes and Proceedings . . . of Congress? *Both the First and Second Continental Congresses consistently published their state papers as soon as they adopted them. That the Bill of Rights, a document which many members regarded as of premier importance, was not published until October 27 suggests that it may not have been completed until shortly before that date.*

The Association supplies another prop for this argument. It was adopted on October 18, yet the grievances which it enumerates are fewer than those cited in the official List of Grievances. It omits the Currency Act of 1764, the Post Office Act of 1765, and the Quartering

Act of 1774. This fact suggests that as of October 18 Congress had not yet established a complete list of grievances; the Bill of Rights and List of Grievances may, in other words, still have been under discussion on that date.

The evidence seems to suggest, then, that the Bill of Rights was not completed until after October 18, and perhaps not until shortly before Congress adjourned on October 26.

WHEREAS, since the close of the laſt war, the British parliament claiming a power, of right to bind the people of America, by ſtatute in all cases whatsoever, hath in some acts expressly imposed taxes on them, and in others under various pretences, but in faƈt for the purpose of raising a revenue, hath imposed rates and duties payable in these colonies, eſtablished a board of commissioners with unconſtitutional powers, and extended the jurisdiƈtion of courts of admiralty, not only for colleƈting the said duties, but for the trial of causes merely arising within the body of a county.

AND whereas in consequence of other ſtatutes, judges, who before held only eſtates at will in their offices, have been made dependant on the crown alone for their salaries, and ſtanding armies kept in time of peace. And it has lately been resolved in parliament, that by force of a ſtatute, made in the thirty-fifth year of the reign of King Henry the eighth, coloniſts may be transported to England and tried there upon accusations for treasons and misprisions, or concealments of treasons committed in the colonies; and by a late ſtatute, such trials have been direƈted in cases therein mentioned.

AND whereas in the laſt session of parliament, three ſtatutes were made: one entitled, "An aƈt to discontinue in such manner, and for such time as are therein mentioned, the landing and discharging, lading or shipping of goods, wares and merchandize, at the town, and within the harbour of Boſton, in the province of Massachusetts-Bay, in North-America." Another entitled, "An aƈt for the better regulating the government of the province of the Massachusetts-Bay, in New-

England." And another entitled, "An act for the impartial administration of justice, in the cases of persons questioned for any act done by them in the execution of the law, or for the suppression of riots and tumults, in the province of the Massachusetts-Bay, in New-England." And another statute was then made, "for making more effectual provision for the government of the province of Quebec, &c." All which statutes are impolitic, unjust, and cruel, as well as unconstitutional, and most dangerous and destructive of American rights.

AND whereas, assemblies have been frequently dissolved, contrary to the rights of the people, when they attempted to deliberate on grievances; and their dutiful, humble, loyal and reasonable petitions to the crown for redress, have been repeatedly treated with contempt by his Majesty's ministers of state.

THE good people of the several colonies of New-Hampshire, Massachusetts-Bay, Rhode-Island and Providence plantations, Connecticut, New-York, New-Jersey, Pennsylvania, New-Castle Kent and Sussex on Delaware, Maryland, Virginia, North-Carolina, and South-Carolina, justly alarmed at these arbitrary proceedings of parliament and administration, have severally elected, constituted, and appointed deputies to meet and sit in general congress in the city of Philadelphia, in order to obtain such establishment, as that their religion, laws, and liberties may not be subverted: Whereupon the deputies so appointed being now assembled, in a full and free representation of these colonies, taking into their most serious consideration the best means of attaining the ends aforesaid, do in the firstplace, as Englishmen their ancestors in like cases have usually done, for asserting and vindicating their rights and liberties, DECLARE,

THAT the inhabitants of the English colonies in North-America, by the immutable laws of nature, the principles of the English constitution, and the several charters or compacts, have the following RIGHTS.—

Resolved, N. C. D. 1. THAT they are entitled to life, liberty, and property: and they have never ceded to any sovereign power whatever, a right to dispose of either without their consent.

Resolved, N. C. D. 2. THAT our ancestors, who first settled these colonies, were at the time of their emigration from the mother country,

53

entitled to all the rights, liberties, and immunities of free and natural born subjects, within the realm of England.

Resolved, N. C. D. 3. THAT by such emigration they by no means forfeited, surrendered, or lost any of those rights, but that they were, and their descendants now are, entitled to the exercise and enjoyment of all such of them, as their local and other circumstances enable them to exercise and enjoy.

Resolved, 4. THAT the foundation of English liberty and of all free government, is a right in the people to participate in their legislative council: and as the English colonists are not represented, and from their local and other circumstances cannot properly be represented in the British parliament, they are entitled to a free and exclusive power of legislation in their several provincial Legislatures, where their right of representation can alone be preserved, in all cases of taxation and internal polity, subject only to the negative of their sovereign, in such manner as has been heretofore used and accustomed: But from the necessity of the case, and a regard to the mutual interests of both countries, we cheerfully consent to the operation of such acts of the British parliament, as are bona fide, restrained to the regulation of our external commerce, for the purpose of securing the commercial advantages of the whole empire to the mother country, and the commercial benefits of its respective members, excluding every idea of taxation internal or external, for raising a revenue on the subjects in America without their consent.

Resolved, N. C. D. 5. THAT the respective colonies are entitled to the common law of England, and more especially to the great and inestimable priviledge of being tried by their peers of the vicinage, according to the course of that law.

Resolved, 6. THAT they are entitled to the benefit of such of the English statutes, as existed at the time of their colonization; and which they have, by experience, respectively found to be applicable to their several local and other circumstances.

Resolved, N. C. D. 7. THAT these, his Majesty's, colonies are likewise entitled to all the immunities and privileges granted and confirmed to them by royal charters, or secured by their several codes of provincial laws.

Resolved, N. C. D. 8. THAT they have a right peaceably to assemble, consider of their grievances, and petition the King; and that all prosecutions, prohibitory proclamations, and commitments for the same, are illegal.

Resolved, N. C. D. 9. THAT the keeping a standing army in these colonies, in times of peace, without the consent of the legislature of that colony in which such army is kept, is against law.

Resolved, N. C. D. 10. IT is indispensibly necessary to good government, and rendered essential by the English constitution, that the constituent branches of the legislature be independent of each other; that, therefore, the exercise of legislative power in several colonies, by a council appointed, during pleasure, by the crown, is unconstitutional, dangerous, and destructive to the freedom of American legislation.

ALL and each of which, the aforesaid deputies in behalf of themselves, and their constituents, do claim, demand, and insist on, as their indubitable rights and liberties; which cannot be legally taken from them, altered or abridged by any power whatever, without their own consent, by their representatives in their several provincial legislatures.

IN the course of our inquiry, we find many infringements and violations of the foregoing rights; which, from an ardent desire that harmony and mutual intercourse of affection and interest may be restored, we pass over for the present, and proceed to state such acts and measures as have been adopted since the last war, which demonstrate a system formed to enslave America.

Resolved, N. C. D. THAT the following acts of parliament are infringements and violations of the rights of the colonists; and that the repeal of them is essentially necessary, in order to restore harmony between Great-Britain and the American colonies, viz.

THE several acts of 4 Geo. III, ch. 15. and ch. 34.—5 Geo. III, ch. 25.—6 Geo. III. ch. 52.—7 Geo. III. ch. 41. and ch. 46.—8 Geo. III. ch. 22. [10] which impose duties for the purpose of raising a revenue in America, extend the powers of the admiralty courts beyond their ancient limits, deprive the American subject of trial by jury, authorise the judges certificate to indemnify the prosecutor from damages, that he might otherwise be liable to, requiring oppressive security from a claimant of ships and goods seized, before he shall be allowed to defend his property, and are subversive of American rights.

ALSO 12 Geo. III. ch. 24. intituled, "An act for the better securing his Majesty's dock-yards, magazines, ships, ammunition and stores." Which declares a new offence in America, and deprives the American subject of a constitutional trial by jury of the vicinage, by authorising the trial of any person charged with the committing any offence described in the said act out of the realm, to be indicted and tried for the same in any shire or county within the realm.

ALSO the three acts passed in the last session of parliament, for stopping the port and blocking up the harbour of Boston, for altering the charter and government of Massachusetts-Bay, and that which is intituled, "An act for the better administration of justice," &c.

ALSO the act passed in the same session for establishing the Roman catholic religion in the province of Quebec, abolishing the equitable system of English laws, and erecting a tyranny there, to the great danger, from so total a dissimularity of religion, law, and government to the neighbouring British colonies, by the assistance of whose blood and treasure the said country was conquered from France.

ALSO the act passed in the same session for the better providing suitable quarters for officers and soldiers in his Majesty's service in North-America.

ALSO, that the keeping a standing army in several of these colonies, in time of peace, without the consent of the legislature of that colony in which such army is kept, is against law.

NOTES

[1] John Adams, *Diary and Autobiography*, ed. Lyman H. Butterfield et al., vol. 3 (Cambridge: Belknap Press of Harvard University Press, 1961), pp. 309–10.

[2] *JCC*, 1:27–29, 42, 63–73.

[3] Diary of Samuel Ward, October 15, 1774, Ward Papers, Rhode Island Historical Society; Burnett, *Letters*, 1:79.

[4] Ibid., p. 75.

[5] Adams, *Diary and Autobiography*, 3:310; Burnett, *Letters*, 1:77.

[6] Adams, *Diary and Autobiography*, 3:310.

[7] John Adams, *The Works of John Adams*, ed. Charles Francis Adams, 10 vols. (Boston: Little and Brown, 1850–56), 2:377n, 535–42.

[8] *JCC*, 1:63–73.

[9] Adams, *Diary and Autobiography*, 2:152–53.

[10] 4 Geo. III, c. 15, was the Sugar Act; 4 Geo. III, c. 34, was the Currency Act of 1764; 5 Geo. III. c. 25, was "An act to alter certain rates of postage, and to amend, explain, and enlarge several provisions in an act made in the ninth year of the reign of Queen Anne . . ."; 6 Geo. III, c. 52, was the Revenue Act of 1766; 7 Geo. III, c. 41, authorized the creation of an American board of customs commissioners; 7 Geo. III, c. 46, levied the Townshend Duties; 8 Geo. III, c. 22, "an act for the more easy and effectual recovery of the penalties and forfeitures inflicted by the acts of parliament relating to the trade and revenues of the British colonies and plantations in America," authorized the establishment of additional vice-admiralty courts in North America and gave them original jurisdiction in their districts. Danby Pickering, ed., *The Statutes at Large* . . . (Cambridge, 1762–1869), 26 (1764): 33–52, 103–5; 26 (1765): 249–60; 27 (1766): 275–87; 27 (1767): 445–49, 505–17; 28 (1768): 70–71.
Of these acts, 5 Geo. III, c. 25, will rarely be found in any scholarly account of American grievances. Drawn with the blessing Benjamin Franklin, it amended the Post Office Act of 1710 by lowering rates in North America. The Post Office was an issue of some constitutional importance in the Anglo-American quarrel. Apologists for the British ministry occasionally cited it to show the inconsistency of the American position on parliamentary taxation. Americans, they said, accepted the Post Office Act of 1710, in which Parliament imposed fees upon them, yet fulminated against other revenue measures like the Stamp Act. Where was their logic? Certain delegates to the First Continental Congress, James Duane, for example, apparently wanted to identify the Post Office Act of 1710 as an official grievance, but the decision of Congress to protest no British measures before 1763 frustrated their efforts. By protesting the Post Office Act of 1765, which was written to amend the Post Office Act of 1710, Congress was evidently attempting to circumvent the 1763 limitation and register its objections to the 1710 Act. Burnett, *Letters*, 1:53, 85; *JCC*, 1:42; Benjamin Franklin, *The Papers of Benjamin Franklin*, ed, Leonard W. Labaree, vol. 11 (New Haven: Yale University Press, 1967), pp. 535–36.

A Letter to the Inhabitants
of the Province of Quebec

Philadelphia: Printed by
William and Thomas Bradford,
October, 1774

On October 21, 1774, Congress resolved to prepare an address to the people of Quebec. John Dickinson, Richard Henry Lee, and Thomas Cushing were appointed a committee to write it. The committee reported a draft on October 24 which was debated and recommitted. On October 26 a revised draft was reported and approved.[1]

In the Library Company of Philadelphia there is a draft of the address, closely approximating the version approved on October 26, in John Dickinson's hand. Whether this was the first draft or the second cannot now be determined. It is possible, of course, that Dickinson's draft is merely a fair copy of someone else's work, but since the Farmer was not accustomed to serving as another man's amanuensis, it is probably safe to credit him with the composition of the address. On October 4, 1774, John Adams recorded in his diary that Charles Lee, an ex-British army officer who was in Philadelphia hovering around the edges of the Continental Congress, showed him "an Address from the C[ongress] to the People of Canada," but what use, if any, was made of Lee's lucubration is not known.[2]

The Bradfords printed the Letter, as the address was called, separately, with a title page bearing the date October 1774, but they numbered the first page 37, indicating that they expected their customers to bind it with the Extracts From the Votes and Proceedings of . . . Congress, the last page of which was numbered 36. After adopting the Letter on October 26, Congress instructed the Pennsylvania delegation to have it translated into French and, with the assistance of the New York, Massachusetts, and New Hampshire delegations, to distribute it.[3] The Pennsylvanians commissioned Pierre Du Simitière, a Swiss-born artist and naturalist residing in Philadelphia, to translate it and Fleury Mesplet to print 2,000 copies. In mid-November 300 copies were sent to Boston by ship for distribution in Canada.[4] General Carleton's correspondence shows that the Letter circulated in Canada. Apparently it had some influence in promoting the efforts of the British residents of Montreal to send delegates to the Second Continental Congress.[5]

W E, the DELEGATES of the Colonies of New-Hampshire, Massachusetts-Bay, Rhode-Island and Providence Plantations, Connecticut, New-York, New-Jersey, Pennsylvania, The Counties of Newcastle Kent and Sussex on Delaware, Maryland, Virginia, North-Carolina and South-Carolina, deputed by the inhabitants of the said Colonies, to represent them in a General Congress at Philadelphia, in the province of Pennsylvania, to consult together concerning the best methods to obtain redress of our afflicting grievances, having accordingly assembled, and taken into our most serious consideration the state of public affairs on this continent, have thought proper to address your province, as a member therein deeply interested.

WHEN the fortune of war, after a gallant and glorious resistance, had incorporated you with the body of English subjects, we rejoiced in the truly valuable addition, both on our own and your account; expecting, as courage and generosity are naturally united, our brave enemies would become our hearty friends, and that the Divine Being would bless to you the dispensations of his over-ruling providence, by securing to you and your latest posterity the inestimable advantages of a free English constitution of government, which it is the privilege of all English subjects to enjoy.

THESE hopes were confirmed by the King's proclamation, issued in the year 1763, plighting the public faith for your full enjoyment of those advantages.

LITTLE did we imagine that any succeeding Ministers would so audaciously and cruelly abuse the royal authority, as to with-hold from you the fruition of the irrevocable rights, to which you were thus justly entitled.

BUT since we have lived to see the unexpected time, when Ministers of this flagitious temper have dared to violate the most sacred compacts and obligations, and as you, educated under another form of government, have artfully been kept from discovering the unspeakable worth of *that* form you are now undoubtedly entitled to, we esteem it our duty, for the weighty reasons herein after mentioned, to explain to you some of its most important branches.

"In every human society," says the celebrated Marquis *Beccaria,* "there is an *effort, continually tending* to confer on one part the heighth of power and happiness, and to reduce the other to the extreme of weakness and misery. The intent of good laws is to *oppose this effort,* and to diffuse their influence *universally* and *equally.*"

Rulers, stimulated by this pernicious "effort," and subjects, animated by the just "intent of opposing good laws against it," have occasioned that vast variety of events, that fill the histories of so many nations. All these histories demonstrate the truth of this simple position, that to live by the will of one man, or sett of men, is the production of misery to all men.

On the solid foundation of this principle, Englishmen reared up the fabrick of their constitution with such a strength, as for ages to defy time, tyranny, treachery, internal and foreign wars: And, as an illustrious author * of your nation, hereafter mentioned, observes,—"They gave the people of their Colonies the form of their own government, and this government carrying prosperity along with it, they have grown great nations in the forests they were sent to inhabit."

In this form, the first grand right is, that of the people having a share in their own government, by their representatives, chosen by themselves, and in consequence of being ruled by *laws* which they themselves approve, not by *edicts* of *men* over whom they have no controul. This is a bulwark surrounding and defending their property, which by their honest cares and labours they have acquired, so that no portions of it can legally be taken from them, but with their own full and free consent, when they in their judgment deem it just and necessary to give them for public services, and precisely direct the easiest, cheapest, and most equal methods, in which they shall be collected.

The influence of this right extends still farther. If money is wanted by Rulers who have in any manner oppressed the people, they may retain it, until their grievances are redressed; and thus peaceably procure

* Montesquieu.[6]

relief, without trusting to despised petitions, or disturbing the public tranquility.

THE next great right is, that of trial by jury. This provides, that neither life, liberty nor property can be taken from the possessor, until twelve of his unexceptionable countrymen and peers, of his vicinage, who from that neighbourhood may reasonably be supposed to be acquainted with his character, and the characters of the witnesses, upon a fair trial, and full enquiry, face to face, in open Court, before as many of the people as chuse to attend, shall pass their sentence upon oath against him; a sentence that cannot injure him, without injuring their own reputation, and probably their interest also; as the question may turn on points, that, in some degree, concern the general welfare; and if it does not, their verdict may form a precedent, that, on a similar trial of their own, may militate against themselves.

ANOTHER right relates merely to the liberty of the person. If a subject is seized and imprisoned, tho' by order of Government, he may, by virtue of this right, immediately obtain a writ, termed a Habeas Corpus, from a Judge, whose sworn duty it is to grant it, and thereupon procure any illegal restraint to be quickly enquired into and redressed.

A FOURTH right is, that of holding lands by the tenure of easy rents, and not by rigorous and oppressive services, frequently forcing the possessors from their families and their business, to perform what ought to be done, in all well regulated states, by men hired for the purpose.

THE last right we shall mention, regards the freedom of the press. The importance of this consists, besides the advancement of truth, science, morality, and arts in general, in its diffusion of liberal sentiments on the administration of Government, its ready communication of thoughts between subjects, and its consequential promotion of union among them, whereby oppressive officers are shamed or intimidated into more honourable and just modes of conducting affairs.

THESE are the invaluable rights, that form a considerable part of our mild system of government; that, sending its equitable energy through all ranks and classes of men, defends the poor from the rich, the weak from the powerful, the industrious from the rapacious, the peaceable from the violent, the tenants from the lords, and all from their superiors.

THESE are the rights, without which a people cannot be free and happy, and under the protecting and encouraging influence of which, these Colonies have hitherto so amazingly flourished and increased. These are the rights a profligate Ministry are now striving by force of arms, to ravish from us, and which we are, with one mind, resolved never to resign but with our lives.

THESE are the rights *you* are entitled to, and ought at this moment in perfection to exercise. And what is offered to you by the late Act of Parliament in their place? Liberty of conscience in your religion? No. God gave it to you; and the temporal powers with which you have been and are connected, firmly stipulated for your enjoyment of it. If laws, divine and human, could secure it against the despotic caprices of wicked men, it was secured before. Are the French laws in *civil* cases restored? *It seems so.* But observe the cautious kindness of the Ministers, who pretend to be your benefactors. The words of the statute are —that those "laws shall be the rule, until they shall be *varied* or *altered* by any ordinances of the Governor and Council." Is the "certainty and lenity of the *criminal* law of England, and its benefits and advantages," commended in the said statute, and said to "have been sensibly felt by you," secured to you and your descendants? No. They too are subjected to arbitrary *"alterations"* by the Governor and Council; and a power is expresly reserved of appointing "such Courts of *criminal, civil* and *ecclesiastical* jurisdiction, as shall be thought proper." Such is the precarious tenure of mere *will*, by which you hold your lives and religion. The Crown and its Ministers are impowered, as far as they could be by Parliament, to establish even the *Inquisition* itself among you. Have you an Assembly composed of worthy men, elected by yourselves, and in whom you can confide, to make laws for you, to watch over your welfare, and to direct in what quantity, and in what manner, your money shall be taken from you? No. The power of making laws for you is lodged in the Governor and Council, all of them dependant upon, and removable at the *pleasure* of a Minister. Besides, another late statute, made without your consent, has subjected you to the impositions of *Excise,* the horror of all free states; thus wresting your property from you by the most odious of taxes, and laying open to insolent tax-gatherers, houses, the scenes of domestic peace and comfort, and called the castles of English subjects in the books of their law. And in the very act for altering your government, and intended to flatter you, you are not authorised to "assess, levy or apply any *rates* and *taxes,* but for the inferior purposes of *making roads,* and erecting and repairing *public buildings,* or for other *local* conveniences, within your respective towns and diſtricts." Why this degrading diſtinction? Ought not the property honeſtly acquired by *Canadians* to be held as sacred as that of *Englishmen?* Have not Canadians sense enough to attend to any other public affairs, than gathering ſtones from one place and piling them up in another? Unhappy people! who are not only injured, but insulted. Nay more!—With such a superlative contempt of your understanding and spirit has an insolent Ministry presumed to think of you, our respectable fellow-subjects, according to the information we have received, as firmly to perswade themselves that your gratitude, for the injuries and insults they have recently offered to you, will engage you to take up arms, and render yourselves the ridicule and deteſtation of the world, by becoming tools, in their hands, to assiſt them in taking that freedom from *us,* which they have treacherously denied to *you;* the unavoidable consequence of which attempt, if successful, would be the extinction of all hopes of you or your poſterity being ever reſtored to freedom: For idiocy itself cannot believe, that, when their drudgery is performed, they will treat you with less cruelty than they have us, who are of the same blood with themselves.

WHAT would your countryman, the immortal *Montesquieu,* have said to such a plan of domination, as has been framed for you? Hear his words, with an intenseness of thought suited to the importance of the subject. [7]—"In a free ſtate, every man, who is supposed a free agent, *ought to be concerned in his own government:* Therefore the *legislative* should reside in the whole body of the *people,* or their *representatives.*"—"The political liberty of the subject is *a tranquillity of mind,* arising from the opinion each person has of his *safety.* In order to have this liberty, it is requisite the government be so conſtituted, as that one man need not be *afraid* of another. When the power of *making* laws, and the power of *executing* them, are *united* in the same person, or in the same body of Magiſtrates, *there can be no liberty;* because apprehensions may arise, leſt the same *Monarch* or *Senate* should enact tyrannical laws, to *execute* them in a tyrannical manner."

"THE power of *judging* should be exercised by persons taken from the *body of the people,* at certain times of the year, and pursuant to a form and manner prescribed by law. *There is no liberty,* if the power of *judging* be not *separated* from the *legislative* and *executive* powers."

65

"MILITARY men belong to a profession, which *may be* useful, but *is often* dangerous."—"The enjoyment of liberty, and even its support and preservation, consists in every man's being allowed to speak his thoughts, and lay open his sentiments."

APPLY these decisive maxims, sanctified by the authority of a name which all Europe reveres, to your own state. You have a Governor, it may be urged, vested with the *executive* powers, or the powers of *administration*. In him, and in your Council, is lodged the power of *making laws*. You have *Judges,* who are to *decide* every cause affecting your lives, liberty or property. Here is, indeed, an appearance of the several powers being *separated* and *distributed* into *different* hands, for checks one upon another, the only effectual mode ever invented by the wit of men, to promote their freedom and prosperity. But scorning to be illuded by a tinsel'd outside, and exerting the natural sagacity of Frenchmen, *examine* the specious device, and you will find it, to use an expression of holy writ, "a whited sepulchre," for burying your lives, liberty and property.

YOUR *Judges,* and your *Legislative Council,* as it is called, are *dependant* on your *Governor,* and *he* is *dependant* on the servant of the Crown in Great Britain. The *legislative, executive* and *judging* powers are *all* moved by the nods of a Minister. Privileges and immunities last no longer than his smiles. When he frowns, their feeble forms dissolve. Such a treacherous ingenuity has been exerted in drawing up the code lately offered you, that every sentence, beginning with a benevolent pretension, concludes with a destructive power; and the substance of the whole, divested of its smooth words, is—that the Crown and its Ministers shall be as absolute throughout your extended province, as the despots of Asia or Africa. What can protect your property from taxing edicts, and the rapacity of necessitous and cruel masters? your persons from Letters de Cachet, goals, dungeons, and oppressive services? your lives and general liberty from arbitrary and unfeeling rulers? We defy you, casting your view upon every side, to discover a single circumstance, promising from any quarter the faintest hope of liberty to you or your posterity, but from an entire adoption into the union of these Colonies.

WHAT advice would the truly great man before mentioned, that advocate of freedom and humanity, give you, was he now living, and knew that we, your numerous and powerful neighbours, animated by

66

a just love of our invaded rights, and united by the indissoluble bands of affection and interest, called upon you, by every obligation of regard for yourselves and your children, as we now do, to join us in our righteous contest, to make common cause with us therein, and take a noble chance for emerging from a humiliating subjection under Governors, Intendants, and Military Tyrants, into the firm rank and condition of English freemen, whose custom it is, derived from their ancestors, to make those tremble, who dare to think of making them miserable?

WOULD not this be the purport of his address? "Seize the opportunity presented to you by Providence itself. You have been conquered into liberty, if you act as you ought. This work is not of man. You are a small people, compared to those who with open arms invite you into a fellowship. A moment's reflection should convince you which will be most for your interest and happiness, to have all the rest of North-America your unalterable friends, or your inveterate enemies. The injuries of Boston have roused and associated every colony, from Nova-Scotia to Georgia. Your province is the only link wanting to compleat the bright and strong chain of union. Nature has joined your country to theirs. Do you join your political interests. For their own sakes, they never will desert or betray you. Be assured, that the happiness of a people inevitably depends on their liberty, and their spirit to assert it. The value and extent of the advantages tendered to you are immense. Heaven grant you may not discover them to be blessings after they have bid you an eternal adieu."

WE are too well acquainted with the liberality of sentiment distinguishing your nation, to imagine, that difference of religion will prejudice you against a hearty amity with us. You know, that the transcendant nature of freedom elevates those, who unite in her cause, above all such low minded infirmities. The Swiss Cantons furnish a memorable proof of this truth. Their union is composed of Roman Catholic and Protestant States, living in the utmost concord and peace with one another, and thereby enabled, ever since they bravely vindicated their freedom, to defy and defeat every tyrant that has invaded them.

SHOULD there be any among you, as there generally are in all societies, who prefer the favours of Ministers, and their own private interests, to the welfare of their country, the temper of such selfish persons will render them incredibly active in opposing all public-spirited measures, from an expectation of being well rewarded for their sordid industry, by their superiors; but we doubt not you will be upon your guard against such men, and not sacrifice the liberty and happiness of the whole Canadian people and their posterity, to gratify the avarice and ambition of individuals.

We do not ask you, by this address, to commence acts of hostility against the government of our common Sovereign. We only invite you to consult your own glory and welfare, and not to suffer yourselves to be inveigled or intimidated by infamous Ministers so far, as to become the instruments of their cruelty and despotism, but to unite with us in one social compact, formed on the generous principles of equal liberty, and cemented by such an exchange of beneficial and endearing offices as to render it perpetual. In order to complete this highly desirable union, we submit to your consideration, whether it may not be expedient for you to meet together in your several towns and districts, and elect Deputies, who afterwards meeting in a provincial Congress, may chuse Delegates, to represent your province in the continental Congress to be held at Philadelphia on the tenth day of May, 1775.

In this present Congress, beginning on the fifth day of the last month, and continued to this day, it has been, with universal pleasure and an unanimous vote, resolved, That we should consider the violation of your rights, by the act for altering the government of your province, as a violation of our own, and that you should be invited to accede to our confederation, which has no other objects than the perfect security of the natural and civil rights of all the constituent members, according to their respective circumstances, and the preservation of a happy and lasting connection with Great-Britain, on the salutary and constitutional principles herein before mentioned. For effecting these purposes, we have addressed an humble and loyal petition to his Majesty, praying relief of our and your grievances; and have associated to stop all importations from Great-Britain and Ireland, after the first day of December, and all exportations to those Kingdoms and the West-Indies, after the tenth day of next September, unless the said grievances are redressed.

That Almighty God may incline your minds to approve our equitable and necessary measures, to add yourselves to us, to put your fate, whenever you suffer injuries which you are determined to oppose, not on the small influence of your single province, but on the consolidated powers of North-America, and may grant to our joint exertions an event as happy as our cause is juſt, is the fervent prayer of us, your sincere and affectionate friends and fellow-subjects.

By order of the Congress,

HENRY MIDDLETON, President.

October 26, 1774.

NOTES

[1] *JCC,* 1:101, 103, 105.

[2] John Adams, *Diary and Autobiography,* ed. Lyman H. Butterfield et al., vol. 2 (Cambridge, Belknap Press of Harvard University Press, 1961), p. 147.

[3] *JCC,* 1:113.

[4] Ibid., p. 122.

[5] Victor Coffin, *The Province of Quebec and the Early American Revolution,* Bulletin of the University of Wisconsin, History Series (Madison, Wis., 1896), pp. 485, 496.

[6] The quotation is from M. de Secondat, Baron de Montesquieu, *The Spirit of the Laws,* trans. Thomas Nugent (London: Printed for J. Collingwood et al. by T. C. Hansard, 1823), vol. 1 (book 19, chapter 27), p. 318.

[7] The following quotations are from Montesquieu's famous description entitled "Of the Constitution of England." Ibid. (book 11, chapter 6), pp. 152–61.

Petition to the King

Printed from
Dunlap's Pennsylvania Packet,
Supplement, January 17, 1775

On October 1, 1774, Congress resolved that "a loyal address to his Majesty be prepared" and appointed Richard Henry Lee, John Adams, Thomas Johnson, Patrick Henry, and John Rutledge a committee to compose it. The committee reported a draft on October 21 which was considered and recommitted; Congress then added John Dickinson to the committee. On October 24 a new draft was reported which was debated and approved the next day. The authorship of the Address to the King, or Petition as it was commonly called, has been exhaustively explored recently by Edwin Wolf 2d, who convincingly demonstrates that Dickinson was the draftsman of the version adopted by Congress on October 25.[1]

On October 26 Congress approved a letter to the agents of all the American colonies in London, ordering them to present the petition to the king and, after presentation, to make it public.[2] *Secretary Charles Thomson forthwith sent, by different ships, two engrossed copies, signed by all the members, to Benjamin Franklin, who was agent for four of the colonies.*[3] *Franklin received the petitions in mid-December and immediately called a meeting of the agents to decide how to proceed. For various reasons only the Doctor and two colleagues, Arthur Lee and William Bollan, were willing to take the responsibility for presenting the petition, which they did through Lord Dartmouth, secretary of state for America, on December 21, 1774.*[4] *The king, Dartmouth replied, "was pleas'd to receive it very graciously and to promise to lay it, as soon as they met, before his two Houses of Parliament."*[5]

Franklin reported to Thomson on February 5, 1775, that he, Lee, and Bollan then consulted on the publication of the petition and "were advised by wise and able men, Friends of America, whose names it would not be proper to mention, by no means to publish it till it should be before Parliament, as it would be deemed disrespectful to the King."[6] *Since Parliament was not scheduled to meet until January 19, 1775, the agents evidently intended to do nothing until after that date, but their hands were forced when the petition was leaked to the London publisher Thomas Becket, who published it at the end of the second week of January 1775 in a collection entitled* Authentic Papers From America: Submitted to the Dispassionate Consideration of the Public.[7]

Becket's miscellany was introduced by a writer who signed himself "Impartial" but who, judging from the tenor of his preface and footnotes, was no uncritical admirer of America. Impartial's object was to show that the controversy with the colonies was not, as some Britishers assumed, "a local effect from the late Acts of Parliament, remediable by repealing them." To make his point he interleaved the petition of the Continental Congress with the petitions of the Stamp Act Congress to the king, the House of Lords, and the House of Commons; that is, a page of the 1774 petition was printed facing a page of the 1765 petitions and this arrangement was continued until the documents concluded. Added to the petitions were the Continental Congress' Address to the People of Great Britain, Congress' letter to the agents of October 26, 1774, and a few lesser documents generated by the imperial quarrel.

Franklin, Lee, and Bollan were patently unhappy with the premature publication of the petition and on January 17, 1775, wrote the following letter, which appeared in the Gazetteer *on January 18, 1775:*

A Copy of the Petition to the King, from the General Congress in America, having been published in a pamphlet printed for T. Becket in the Strand, we, to whom the care of presenting and publishing that petition was committed by the Congress, think it our duty to inform the public, that the above mentioned copy is surreptitious, as well as materially and grossly erroneous. The agents have deferred the making the Petition public out of respect to the King and the Parliament, his Majesty having declared his intentions of having it laid before the two Houses of Parliament as soon as they meet.

Becket replied in the January 19–21, 1775, issue of the London Chronicle:

The Publisher of a Pamphlet under the title of "Authentic Papers from America," has been attacked by a redoubtable triumvirate of Gentlemen, who deny the authenticity of the Petition from the General Congress to the King. Their authority in the case should be uncontrovertible; Yet the Publisher takes upon him to say that his is undoubted. He did not know their reasons for suspending the publication, contrary to the instruction in the letter conveying the Petition to them, which was sent to him in an American Paper. A few days will decide between the publication and the denial of these Gentlemen: And the Publisher will readily refund the money for every copy bought on this and the succeeding days, if it should be found to be not genuine.

The issue was submitted to the public's adjudication on January 21, 1775, when the agents published the petition in the London Chronicle. *Shortly thereafter, John Almon published it at the end of an edition of the* Journals of the Continental Congress, *with a prefatory note, dated January 17, 1775, from Franklin, Lee, and Bollan, affirming its authenticity.*[8]

A comparison of the petition published by Becket with those published in the London Chronicle *and by Almon shows that the three are virtually identical and that Becket was correct in claiming that his was "undoubted." His paragraph indentations and italics are different and he omits the list of signers, but the texts of the three are the same in almost all other respects. They agree even in containing the same minor variations from the two signed, engrossed copies sent to Franklin by Thomson; these variations, in fact, provide a clue to how Impartial obtained a copy of the petition.*

When Franklin received the signed, engrossed copies from Thomson in December, he evidently ordered a clerk to make one or more copies which he could use in the various conferences which he foresaw would take place. One of the Doctor's "working copies" is in the Franklin Papers at the Library of Congress. In two places, noticed by Wolf in his study of the petition, it differs from the engrossed copies: a "the" is added at one point, and "colonists" is changed to "colonies" at another.[9] Since both of these changes appear in the Becket, Almon, and London Chronicle *printings, the petition which Impartial supplied to Becket must have been based on Franklin's working copy. Impartial may, therefore, have been a person Franklin consulted about the petition, possibly one of the agents who declined to present it, or perhaps Chatham, Camden, Howe, or someone associated with them.[10]*

The publishing history of the petition in America is far less complicated. Congress declined to authorize its publication immediately after its adoption, because, as the New York delegates wrote their constituents on November 7, 1774, it "cannot in point of Decorum be made publick until it has been laid before the Throne." [11] *By the middle of January 1775 Secretary Thomson, perhaps by prearrangement or perhaps in consultation with the Pennsylvania delegates, who may have concluded that sufficient time had elapsed for the presentation of the petition to the king, distributed copies of it to the Philadelphia newspapers. The* Pennsylvania Packet *scooped its competitors by publishing the petition in a special supplement on January 17, 1775. The* Pennsylvania Journal *and the* Pennsylvania Gazette *published it the next day.*[12] *That the* Packet *published the petition on the very day Franklin, Lee, and Bollan wrote a note vouching for its authenticity in Almon's printing seems to be coincidental, although it is possible that a concert about publication, of which we are ignorant, existed between the agents and Thomson.*

On February 4, 1775, the Bradfords advertised that they had published the petition as an addendum to the Journals of Congress. *Printers in other colonies rapidly reprinted it and by the spring of 1775 people throughout America were familiar with it.*

To the Kings Most Excellent Majesty.

Most Gracious Sovereign,

WE your majestys faithful subjects of the colonies of Newhamp-
shire, Massachusetts-bay, Rhode-island and Providence Plantations, Connecticut, New-York, New-Jersey, Pennsylvania, the counties of
New-Castle Kent and Sussex on Delaware, Maryland, Virginia, North-
Carolina, and South Carolina, in behalf of ourselves and the inhabitants
of these colonies who have deputed us to represent them in General
Congress, by this our humble petition, beg leave to lay our grievances
before the throne.

A standing army has been kept in these colonies, ever since the conclusion of the late war, without the consent of our assemblies; and this army
with a considerable naval armament has been employed to enforce the
collection of taxes.

The Authority of the commander in chief, and, under him, of the
brigadiers general has in time of peace, been rendered supreme in all
the civil governments in America.

The commander in chief of all your majesty's forces in North-America
has, in time of peace, been appointed governor of a colony.

The charges of usual offices have been greatly increased; and, new,
expensive and oppressive offices have been multiplied.

The judges of admiralty and vice-admiralty courts are empowered to
receive their salaries and fees from the effects condemned by themselves.
The officers of the customs are empowered to break open and enter
houses without the authority of any civil magistrate founded on legal
information.

The judges of courts of common law have been made entirely dependant on one part of the legislature for their salaries, as well as for the
duration of their commissions.

Councellors holding their commissions, during pleasure, exercise
legislative authority.

Humble and reasonable petitions from the representatives of the people
have been fruitless.

The agents of the people have been discountenanced and governors
have been instructed to prevent the payment of their salaries.

Assemblies have been repeatedly and injuriously dissolved.

Commerce has been burthened with many useless and oppressive restrictions.

By several acts of parliament made in the fourth, fifth, sixth, seventh, and eighth years of your majestys reign, duties are imposed on us, for the purpose of raising a revenue, and the powers of admiralty and vice-admiralty courts are extended beyond their ancient limits, whereby our property is taken from us without our consent, the trial by jury in many civil cases is abolished, enormous forfeitures are incurred for slight offences, vexatious informers are exempted from paying damages, to which they are justly liable, and oppressive security is required from owners before they are allowed to defend their right.

Both houses of parliament have resolved that colonists may be tried in England, for offences alledged to have been committed in America, by virtue of a statute passed in the thirty fifth year of Henry the eighth; and in consequence thereof, attempts have been made to enforce that statute. A statute was passed in the twelfth year of your majesty's reign, directing, that persons charged with committing any offence therein described, in any place out of the realm, may be indicted and tried for the same, in any shire or county within the realm, whereby inhabitants of these colonies may, in sundry cases by that statute made capital, be deprived of a trial by their peers of the vicinage.

In the last sessions of parliament, an act was passed for blocking up the harbour of Boston; another, empowering the governor of the Massachusetts-bay to send persons indicted for murder in that province to another colony or even to Great Britain for trial whereby such offenders may escape legal punishment; a third, for altering the chartered constitution of government in that province; and a fourth for extending the limits of Quebec, abolishing the English and restoring the French laws, whereby great numbers of British freemen are subjected to the latter, and establishing an absolute government and the Roman Catholick religion throughout those vast regions, that border on the westerly and northerly boundaries of the free protestant English settlements; and a fifth for the better providing suitable quarters for officers and soldiers in his majesty's service in North-America.

To a sovereign, who "glories in the name of Briton" the bare recital of these acts must we presume, justify the loyal subjects, who fly to the foot of his throne and implore his clemency for protection against them.

From this destructive system of colony administration adopted since the conclusion of the last war, have flowed those distresses, dangers, fears and jealousies, that overwhelm your majesty's dutiful colonists with affliction; and we defy our most subtle and inveterate enemies, to trace the unhappy differences between Great-Britain and these colonies, from an earlier period or from other causes than we have assigned. Had they proceeded on our part from a restless levity of temper, unjust impulses of ambition, or artful suggestions of seditious persons, we should merit the opprobrious terms frequently bestowed upon us, by those we revere. But so far from promoting innovations, we have only opposed them; and can be charged with no offence, unless it be one, to receive injuries and be sensible of them.

Had our creator been pleased to give us existence in a land of slavery, the sense of our condition might have been mitigated by ignorance and habit. But thanks be to his adoreable goodness, we were born the heirs of freedom, and ever enjoyed our right under the auspices of your royal ancestors, whose family was seated on the British throne, to rescue and secure a pious and gallant nation from the popery and despotism of a superstitious and inexorable tyrant. Your majesty, we are confident, justly rejoices, that your title to the crown is thus founded on the title of your people to liberty; and therefore we doubt not, but your royal wisdom must approve the sensibility, that teaches your subjects anxiously to guard the blessings, they received from divine providence, and thereby to prove the performance of that compact, which elevated the illustrious house of Brunswick to the imperial dignity it now possesses.

The apprehension of being degraded into a state of servitude from the pre-eminent rank of English freemen, while our minds retain the strongest love of liberty, and clearly foresee the miseries preparing for us and our posterity, excites emotions in our breasts, which though we cannot describe, we should not wish to conceal. Feeling as men, and thinking as subjects, in the manner we do, silence would be disloyalty. By giving this faithful information, we do all in our power, to promote the great objects of your royal cares, the tranquility of your government, and the welfare of your people.

Duty to your majesty and regard for the preservation of ourselves and our posterity, the primary obligations of nature and society command us to entreat your royal attention; and as your majesty enjoys the signal distinction of reigning over freemen, we apprehend the language of freemen can not be displeasing. Your royal indignation, we hope, will rather fall on those designing and dangerous men, who daringly interposing themselves between your royal person and your faithful subjects, and for several years past incessantly employed to dissolve the bonds of society, by abusing your majesty's authority, misrepresenting your American subjects and prosecuting the most desperate and irritating projects of oppression, have at length compelled us, by the force of accumulated injuries too severe to be any longer tolerable, to disturb your majesty's repose by our complaints.

These sentiments are extorted from hearts, that much more willingly would bleed in your majesty's service. Yet so greatly have we been misrepresented, that a necessity has been alledged of taking our property from us without our consent "to defray the charge of the administration of justice, the support of civil government, and the defence protection and security of the colonies." But we beg leave to assure your majesty, that such provision has been and will be made for defraying the two first articles, as has been and shall be judged, by the legislatures of the several colonies, just and suitable to their respective circumstances: And for the defence protection and security of the colonies, their militias, if properly regulated, as they earnestly desire may immediately be done, would be fully sufficient, at least in times of peace; and in case of war, your faithful colonists will be ready and willing, as they ever have been when constitutionally required, to demonstrate their loyalty to your majesty, by exerting their most strenuous efforts in granting supplies and raising forces. Yielding to no British subjects, in affectionate attachment to your majesty's person, family and government, we too dearly prize the privilege of expressing that attachment by those proofs, that are honourable to the prince who receives them, and to the people who give them, ever to resign it to any body of men upon earth.

Had we been permitted to enjoy in quiet the inheritance left us by our forefathers, we should at this time have been peaceably, cheerfully and usefully employed in recommending ourselves by every testimony of devotion to your majesty, and of veneration to the state, from which we derive our origin. But though now exposed to unexpected and unnatural scenes of distress by a contention with that nation, in whose parental guidance on all important affairs we have hitherto with filial reverence constantly trusted, and therefore can derive no instruction in our present unhappy and perplexing circumstances from any former experience, yet we doubt not, the purity of our intention and the integrity of our conduct will justify us at that grand tribunal, before which all mankind must submit to judgment,

We ask but for peace, liberty, and safety. We wish not a diminution of the prerogative, nor do we solicit the grant of any new right in our favour. Your royal authority over us and our connexion with Great-

Britain, we shall always carefully and zealously endeavour to support and maintain.

Filled with sentiments of duty to your majesty, and of affection to our parent state, deeply impressed by our education and strongly confirmed by our reason, and anxious to evince the sincerity of these dispositions, we present this petition only to obtain redress of grievances and relief from fears and jealousies occasioned by the system of statutes and regulations adopted since the close of the late war, for raising a revenue in America—extending the powers of courts of admiralty and vice-admiralty—trying persons in Great Britain for offences alledged to be committed in America—affecting the province of Massachusetts-bay, and altering the government and extending the limits of Quebec; by the abolition of which system, the harmony between Great-Britain and these colonies so necessary to the happiness of both and so ardently desired by the latter, and the usual intercourses will be immediately restored. In the magnanimity and justice of your majesty and parliament we confide, for a redress of our other grievances, trusting, that when the causes of our apprehensions are removed, our future conduct will prove us not unworthy of the regard, we have been accustomed, in our happier days, to enjoy. For appealing to that being who searches thoroughly the hearts of his creatures, we solemnly profess, that our councils have been influenced by no other motive, than a dread of impending destruction.

Permit us then, most gracious sovereign, in the name of all your faithful people in America, with the utmost humility to implore you, for the honour of Almighty God, whose pure religion our enemies are undermining; for your glory, which can be advanced only by rendering your subjects happy and keeping them united; for the interests of your family depending on an adherence to the principles that enthroned it; for the safety and welfare of your kingdoms and dominions threatened with almost unavoidable dangers and distresses; that your majesty, as the loving father of your whole people, connected by the same bands of law, loyalty, faith and blood, though dwelling in various countries, will not suffer the transcendant relation formed by these ties to be farther violated, in uncertain expectation of effects, that, if attained, never can compensate for the calamities, through which they must be gained.

We therefore most earnestly beseech your majesty, that your royal authority and interposition may be used for our relief; and that a gracious answer may be given to this petition.

That your majesty may enjoy every felicity through a long and glorious reign over loyal and happy subjects, and that your descendants may inherit your prosperity and dominions 'til time shall be no more, is and always will be our sincere and fervent prayer.

Henry Middleton	John Dickinson
Jn° Sullivan	John Morton
Nath¹. Folsom	Thomas Mifflin
Thomas Cushing	George Ross
Samuel Adams	Chaˢ Humphreys
John Adams	Cæsar Rodney
Robᵗ. Treat Paine	Thoˢ M: Kean
Step Hopkins	Geo: Read
Sam: Ward	Mat. Tilghman
Elipht Dyer	Thˢ. Johnson Junʳ
Roger Sherman	Wᵐ. Paca
Silas Deane	Samuel Chase
Phil. Livingſton	Richard Henry Lee
John Alsop	Patrick Henry
Isaac Low	G°. Washington
Jas. Duane	Edmund Pendleton
John Jay	Richᵈ. Bland
Wᵐ. Floyd	Benjⁿ Harrison
Henry Wisner	Will Hooper
S: Bœrum	Joseph Hewes
Wil: Livingſton	Rᵈ. Caswell
John De Hart	Tho Lynch
Stepⁿ. Crane	Chrisᵗ Gadsden
Richᵈ. Smith	J. Rutledge
E Biddle	Edward Rutledge
J: Galloway	

NOTES

1 Edwin Wolf 2d, "The Authorship of the 1774 Address to the King Restudied," *William and Mary Quarterly*, 3d ser. 22 (April 1965): 189–224.

2 *JCC*, 1:104–5.

3 Wolf, "Authorship," 191–92.

[4] Franklin to Thomson, February 5, 1775, in Benjamin Franklin, *The Writings of Benjamin Franklin,* ed. Albert H. Smyth, vol. 6 (New York: Macmillan, 1907), p. 303; Wolf, "Authorship," pp. 193, 200.

[5] Franklin, "An Account of Negotiations in London," [March 1775], *Writings,* 6:344.

[6] Franklin to Thomson, February 5, 1775, *Writings,* 6:304.

[7] The *London Chronicle,* January 14–17, 1775, announced it as being published "This Day." A preface, written by Impartial, is dated January 10, 1775. The title page of the Library of Congress copy of this extremely rare pamphlet is endorsed "A. Lee," which seems to indicate that it was originally Lee's personal copy.

[8] *Journal of the Proceedings of the Congress, Held at Philadelphia, September 5, 1774* (London: Printed by John Almon, 1775). The Library of Congress copy of this imprint is bound with Almon's 1774 printing of *Extracts From the Votes and Proceedings of . . . Congress.*

[9] Wolf, "Authorship," p. 221.

[10] For Franklin's meetings with these noblemen, see his "Account of Negotiations in London," [March 1775], in *Writings,* 6:347–49, 352.

[11] Burnett, *Letters,* 1:84.

[12] J. H. Powell asserts, without citing specific evidence, that the Bradfords printed two separate editions of the petition in 1774. *The Books of a New Nation, United States Government Publications, 1774–1814* (Philadelphia: University of Pennsylvania Press, 1957), pp. 44–47. Wolf ignores this claim, evidently feeling that it is too unsubstantial to deserve a refutation. I agree with Wolf; I can find no evidence at all for a 1774 printing of the petition. Evans, number 13741, lists what purports to be a Boston 1774 printing of the petition by Isaiah Thomas, but examination of the copy reveals that the date of the imprint and Thomas' name have been added to the title page in an unidentified hand. In fact, this imprint and a Thomas printing of the petition dated 1775 (Evans, number 14555) are identical. A 1775 date would obviously be correct for Evans, number 13741.

To the Oppressed Inhabitants of Canada

Printed from the
Pennsylvania Journal,
June 14, 1775

On May 17, 1775, John Brown of Pittsfield, Mass., arrived in Philadelphia with the news that on May 10 American forces had captured Fort Ticonderoga. The next day Brown, whom the Boston Committee of Correspondence had earlier sent on an intelligence-gathering mission to Montreal,[1] was called before Congress and questioned. He reported that General Guy Carlton had "issued orders for the raising of a Canadian Regiment" to fight the Americans but that it was filling slowly because of the disaffection of the population. The British, he said, were also considering using Indians against the colonists.[2]

On May 26, 1775, after debating the means of countering a British invasion from the north, Congress appointed John Jay, Samuel Adams, and Silas Deane a committee "to prepare and bring in a letter to the people of Canada."[3] The next day James Price, a pro-American merchant from Montreal, was interviewed by Congress about Canadian affairs.[4] Price was returning home soon and evidently offered to carry Congress' letter to his countrymen. On May 27 the committee reported a draft, which was debated and recommitted. On May 29 a new draft, said to have been written by John Jay,[5] was reported, debated, and approved.

The same day, Congress directed John Dickinson and Thomas Mifflin to have the letter translated into French and to have 1,000 copies printed for distribution in Canada.[6] Dickinson and Mifflin engaged the same translator and printer, Du Simitière and Mesplet, who had prepared the First Congress' Letter to Quebec; their combined efforts soon produced the "Lettre addressée aux Habitans opprimés de la Province de Quebec."[7] *On June 12 it was moved in Congress that the* "Lettre" *be published in English.[8] A copy was supplied to the Philadelphia newspapers forthwith and it appeared in the June 14 editions of the* Pennsylvania Journal *and* Pennsylvania Gazette *as a letter addressed "To the Oppressed Inhabitants of Canada."*

FRIENDS AND COUNTRYMEN,

ALARMED by the designs of an arbitrary Miniſtry, to extirpate the Rights and liberties of all America, a sense of common danger conspired with the dictates of humanity, in urging us to call your attention, by our late address, to this very important object.

Since the conclusion of the late war, we have been happy in considering you as fellow-subjects, and from the commencement of the present plan for subjugating the continent, we have viewed you as fellow-sufferers with us. As we were both entitled by the bounty of an indulgent creator to freedom, and being both devoted by the cruel edicts of a despotic adminiſtration, to common ruin, we perceived the fate of the proteſtant and catholic colonies to be ſtrongly linked together, and therefore invited you to join with us in resolving to be free, and in rejecting, with disdain, the fetters of slavery, however artfully polished.

We most sincerely condole with you on the arrival of that day, in the course of which, the sun could not shine on a single freeman in all your extensive dominion. Be assured, that your unmerited degradation has engaged the moſt unfeigned pity of your ſiſter colonies and we flatter ourselves you will not, by tamely bearing the yoke, suffer that pity to be supplanted by contempt.

When hardy attempts are made to deprive men of rights, beſtowed by the almighty, when avenues are cut thro' the moſt solemn compacts for the admission of despotism, when the plighted faith of government ceases to give security to loyal and dutiful subjects, and when the insidious ſtratagems and manœuvres of peace become more terrible than the sanguinary operations of war, it is high time for them to assert those rights, and, with honeſt indignation, oppose the torrent of oppression rushing in upon them.

By the introduction of your present form of government, or rather present form of tyranny, you and your wives and your children are made slaves. You have nothing that you can call your own, and all the fruits of your labour and induſtry may be taken from you, whenever an avaritious governor and a rapacious council may incline to demand them. You are liable by their edicts to be transported into foreign countries to fight Battles in which you have no intereſt, and to spill your blood in conflicts from which neither honor nor emolument can be derived: Nay, the enjoyment of your very religion, on the present system, depends on a legislature in which you have no share, and over which you have no controul, and your priests are exposed to expulsion, banishment, and ruin, whenever their wealth and possessions furnish sufficient temptation They cannot be sure that a virtuous prince will always fill the throne: and should a wicked or a careless king concur with a wicked ministry in extracting the treasure and strength of your country, it is impossible to conceive to what variety and to what extremes of wretchedness you may, under the present establishment, be reduced.

We are informed you have already been called upon to waste your lives in a contest with us. Should you, by complying in this instance, assent to your new establishment, and a war break out with France, your wealth and your sons may be sent to perish in expeditions against their islands in the West indies.

It cannot be presumed that these considerations will have no weight with you, or that you are so lost to all sense of honor. We can never believe that the present race of Canadians are so degenerated as to possess neither the spirit, the gallantry, nor the courage of their ancestors. You certainly will not permit the infamy and disgrace of such pusillanimity to rest on your own heads, and the consequences of it on your children forever.

We, for our parts, are determined to live free, or not at all; and are resolved, that posterity shall never reproach us with having brought slaves into the world.

Permit us again to repeat that we are your friends, not your enemies, and be not imposed upon by those who may endeavour to create animosities. The taking the fort and military stores at Ticonderoga and Crown-Point, and the armed vessels on the lake, was dictated by the great law of self-preservation. They were intended to annoy us and to cut off that friendly intercourse and communication, which has hitherto subsisted between you and us. We hope it has given you no uneasiness, and you may rely on our assurances, that these colonies will pursue no measures whatever, but such as friendship and a regard for our mutual safety and interest may suggest.

As our concern for your welfare entitles us to your friendship, we presume you will not, by doing us injury, reduce us to the disagreeable necessity of treating you as enemies.

We yet entertain hopes of your uniting with us in the defence of our common liberty, and there is yet reason to believe, that should we join in imploring the attention of our sovereign, to the unmerited and unparalleled oppressions of his American subjects, he will at length be undeceived, and forbid a licentious Ministry any longer to riot in the ruins of the rights of Mankind.

NOTES

[1] *Dictionary of American Biography;* Allen French, *The First Year of the American Revolution* (New York: Octagon Books, 1968), pp. 145–46.

[2] Force, *American Archives,* 4th ser., 2:623–24.

[3] *JCC,* 2:64.

[4] Gustave Lanctot, *Canada and the American Revolution, 1774–1783,* trans., Margaret M. Cameron (Toronto: Clarke, Irwin, 1967), pp. 30–31, 46–48.

[5] *JCC,* 2:68.

[6] Ibid., p. 70.

[7] That Du Simitière and Mesplet collaborated on the "Lettre" is asserted in Evans, 5:208. The Library of Congress copy of the "Lettre," which appears in Evans, number 14575, contains on its title page neither the publisher's nor the translator's name. To make their attribution, the compilers of Evans must have received bibliographical information from another source.

[8] On June 1 Congress had resolved "that no expedition or incursion ought to be undertaken or made, by any colony, or body of colonists, against or into Canada; and that this Resolve be immediately transmitted to the commander of the forces at Ticonderoga." It then ordered the resolve translated into French and transmitted, with the "Lettre," to Canada. *JCC,* 2:75.

A Declaration

by the Representatives of the United Colonies of
North-America, now met in GENERAL CONGRESS at
PHILADELPHIA, Seting forth the CAUSES and NECESSITY
of their taking up ARMS

Philadelphia: Printed by
William and Thomas Bradford,
1775

On June 23, 1775, Congress appointed a committee to prepare a declaration "to be published by General Washington upon his arrival at the Camp before Boston." The next day the committee brought in a draft, said to have been written by John Rutledge, which was debated and referred for "farther consideration." The draft was debated again on June 26 and returned to the committee, now reinforced by the addition of Thomas Jefferson and John Dickinson.[1]

In The Papers of Thomas Jefferson, *Julian P. Boyd has masterfully described how Jefferson and Dickinson collaborated to produce the draft of the declaration which Congress approved on July 6, 1775.[2] By this time Congress had decided that the declaration should be brandished before the British as a sword, while it extended, in its other hand, the Olive Branch Petition. Working with their accustomed speed, the Bradfords printed the declaration in pamphlet form by July 8.[3] The next day the Olive Branch Petition, the declaration, and second address to the people of Great Britain were entrusted to Richard Penn as he embarked for London. Penn was ordered to join the American agents residing in the British capital in publishing the latter two documents as "immediately" and "universally" as possible.[4] His ship arrived in Bristol on either August 9 or 13 (reports conflict), and by August 17 he had managed to publish both documents in the London newspapers.[5]*

IF it was possible for men, who exercise their reason to believe, that the Divine Author of our exiſtence intended a part of the human race to hold an absolute property in, and an unbounded power over others, marked out by his infinite goodness and wisdom, as the objects of a legal domination, never rightfully resiſtible, however severe and oppressive, the Inhabitants of these Colonies might at leaſt require from the Parliament of Great-Britain, some evidence, that this dreadful authority over them has been granted to that body. But a reverence for our great Creator, principles of humanity, and the dictates of common sense, muſt convince all those who reflect upon the subject, that government was inſtituted to promote the welfare of mankind, and ought to be adminiſtered for the attainment of that end, The legislature of Great-Britain, however ſtimulated by an inordinate passion for a power not only unjuſtifiable, but which they know to be peculiarly reprobated by the very conſtitution of that kingdom, and desperate of success in any mode of conteſt, where regard should be had to truth, law, or right, have at length, deserting those, attempted to effect their cruel and impolitic purpose of enslaving these Colonies by violence, and have thereby rendered it necessary for us to close with their laſt appeal from Reason to Arms.—Yet, however blinded that assembly may be, by their intemperate rage for unlimited domination, so to slight juſtice and the opinion of mankind, we eſteem ourselves bound by obligations of respect to the reſt of the world, to make known the juſtice of our cause.

OUR forefathers, inhabitants of the island of Great-Britain, left their native land, to seek on these shores a residence for civil and religious freedom. At the expence of their blood, at the hazard of their fortunes, without the leaſt charge to the country from which they removed, by unceasing labor and an unconquerable spirit, they effected settlements in the diſtant and inhospitable wilds of America, then filled with numerous and war-like nations of barbarians.—Societies or governments, veſted with perfect legislatures, were formed under charters from the crown, and an harmonious intercourse was eſtablished between the colonies and the kingdom from which they derived their origin. The mutual benefits of this union became in a short time so extraordinary, as to excite astonishment. It is universally confessed, that the amazing increase of the wealth, strength and navigation of the realm, arose from this source; and the minister who so wisely and successfully directed the measures of Great-Britain in the late war, publicly declared, that these colonies enabled her to triumph over her enemies.—Toward the conclusion of that war, it pleased our sovereign to make a change in his counsel. —From that fatal moment, the affairs of the British empire began to fall into confusion, and gradually sliding from the summit of glorious prosperity to which they had been advanced by the virtues and abilities of one man, are at length distracted by the convulsions, that now shake it to its deepest foundations—The new ministry finding the brave foes of Britain, though frequently defeated, yet still contending, took up the unfortunate idea of granting them a hasty peace, and of then subduing her faithful friends.

THESE devoted colonies were judged to be in such a state, as to present victories without bloodshed, and all the easy emoluments of statuteable plunder.—The uninterrupted tenor of their peaceable and respectful behaviour from the beginning of colonization, their dutiful, zealous and useful services during the war, though so recently and amply acknowledged in the most honorable manner by his Majesty, by the late king, and by Parliament, could not save them from the meditated innovations.—Parliament was influenced to adopt the pernicious project, and assuming a new power over them, have in the course of eleven years given such decisive specimens of the spirit and consequences attending this power, as to leave no doubt concerning the effects of acquiescence under it. They have undertaken to give and grant our money without our consent, though we have ever exercised an exclusive right to dispose of our own property; statutes have been passed for extending the jurisdiction of courts of Admiralty and Vice-Admiralty beyond their ancient limits: for depriving us of the accustomed and inestimable privilege of trial by jury in cases affecting both life and property; for suspending the legislature of one of the colonies; for interdicting all commerce of another; and for altering fundamentally the form of government established by charter, and secured by acts of its own legislature solemnly confirmed by the crown; for exempting the "murderers" of colonists from legal trial, and in effect, from punishment; for erecting in a neighbouring Province, acquired by the joint arms of Great-Britain and America, a despotism dangerous to our very existence; and for quartering soldiers upon the colonists in time of profound peace. It has also been resolved in parliament, that colonists charged with committing certain offences, shall be transported to England to be tried.

BUT why should we enumerate our injuries in detail? By one ftatute it is declared, that parliament can "of right make laws to bind us IN ALL CASES WHATSOEVER." What is to defend us againſt so enormous, so un-limited a power? Not a single man of those who assume it, is chosen by us; or is subject to our controul or influence: but on the contrary, they are all of them exempt from the operation of such laws, and an Ameri-can revenue, if not diverted from the oſtensible purposes for which it is raised, would actually lighten their own burdens in proportion, as they increase ours. We saw the misery to which such despotism would reduce us. We for ten years incessantly and ineffectually besieged the Throne as supplicants; we reasoned, we remonſtrated with parliament in the moſt mild and decent language. But Adminiſtration sensible that we should regard these oppressive measures as freemen ought to do, sent over fleets and armies to enforce them. The indignation of the Americans was roused it is true; but it was the indignation of a virtuous, loyal, and affectionate people. A Congress of Delegates from the united colonies was assembled at Philadelphia, on the fifth day of laſt September. We resolved again to offer an humble and dutiful petition to the king, and also addressed our fellow subjects of Great-Britain. We have pursued every temperate, every respectful measure, we have even proceeded to break off our commercial intercourse with our fellow subjects, as the laſt peaceable admonition, that our attachment to no nation upon earth should supplant our attachment to liberty.—This, we flattered ourselves, was the ultimate ſtep of the controversy: But subsequent events have shewn, how vain was this hope of finding moderation in our enemies.

SEVERAL threatening expression againſt the colonies were inserted in his Majeſty's speech; [6] our petition, though we were told it was a decent one, that his Majeſty had been pleased to receive it graciously, and to promise laying it before his Parliament, was huddled into both houses amongſt a bundle of American papers, and there neglected.[7] The Lords and Commons in their address, in the month of February, said, that "a rebellion at that time actually exiſted within the province of Massachu-setts bay; and that those concerned in it, had been countenanced and encouraged by unlawful combinations and engagements, entered into by his Majeſty's subjects in several of the other colonies; and therefore they besought his Majeſty, that he would take the moſt effectual mea-sures to inforce due obedience to the laws and authority of the supreme legislature" [8]—Soon after the commercial intercourse of whole colonies, with foreign countries and with each other, was cut off by an act of Parliament; by another, several of them were intirely prohibited from the fisheries in the seas near their coasts, on which they always depended for their sustenance; [9] and large re-inforcements of ships and troops were immediately sent over to General Gage.

FRUITLESS were all the entreaties, arguments and eloquence of an illustrious band of the most distinguished Peers and Commoners, who nobly and strenuously asserted the justice of our cause, to stay or even to mitigate the heedless fury with which these accumulated and unexampled outrages were hurried on—Equally fruitless was the interferrence of the city of London, of Bristol, and many other respectable towns in our favour. Parliament adopted an insidious manœuvre [10] calculated to divide us, to establish a perpetual auction of taxations where colony should bid against colony, all of them uninformed what ransom would redeem their lives, and thus to extort from us at the point of the bayonet, the unknown sums that should be sufficient to gratify, if possible to gratify, ministerial rapacity, with the miserable indulgence left to us of raising in our own mode the prescribed tribute. What terms more rigid and humiliating could have been dictated by remorseless victors to conquered enemies? In our circumstances to accept them would be to deserve them.

SOON after the intelligence of these proceedings arrived on this continent, General Gage, who, in the course of the last year, had taken possession of the town of Boston, in the province of Massachusett's-Bay, and still occupied it as a garrison, on the 19th day of April, sent out from that place a large detachment of his army, who made an unprovoked assault on the inhabitants of the said province, at the town of Lexington, as appears by the affidavits of a great number of persons, some of whom were officers and soldiers of that detachment, murdered eight of the inhabitants, and wounded many others. From thence the troops proceeded in warlike array to the town of Concord, where they set upon another party of the inhabitants of the same province, killing several and wounding more, until compelled to retreat by the country people suddenly assembled to repel this cruel aggression. Hostilities thus commenced by the British troops, have been since prosecuted by them without regard to faith or reputation.—The inhabitants of Boston being confined within that town by the General their Governor, and having in order to procure their dismission, entered into a treaty with him, it was stipulated that the said inhabitants having deposited their arms with their own magistrates, should have liberty to depart, taking with them their other effects. They accordingly delivered up their arms, but in open violation of honor, in defiance of the obligation of treaties, which even savage nations esteem sacred, the Governor ordered the arms deposited as aforesaid, that they might be preserved for their owners, to be seized by a body of soldiers; detained the greatest part of the inhabitants in the town, and compelled the few who were permitted to retire, to leave their most valuable effects behind.

By this perfidy, wives are separated from their husbands, children from their parents, the aged and the sick from their relations and friends, who wish to attend and comfort them; and those who have been used to live in plenty, and even elegance, are reduced to deplorable distress.

The General further emulating his ministerial masters, by a proclamation bearing date on the 12th day of June, after venting the grossest falsehoods and calumnies against the good people of these colonies, proceeds to "declare them all either by name or description to be rebels and traitors, to supersede the course of the common law, and instead thereof to publish and order the use and exercise of the law martial."— His troops have butchered our countrymen; have wantonly burnt Charles-Town, besides a considerable number of houses in other places; our ships and vessels are seized; the necessary supplies of provisions are intercepted, and he is exerting his utmost power to spread destruction and devastation around him.

We have received certain intelligence, that General Carleton, the Governor of Canada, is instigating the people of that province and the Indians to fall upon us; and we have but too much reason to apprehend, that schemes have been formed to excite domestic enemies against us. In brief a part of these colonies now feels, and all of them are sure of feeling, as far as the vengeance of administration can inflict them, the complicated calamities of fire, sword and famine.—We are reduced to the alternative of chusing an unconditional submission to the tyranny of irritated ministers or resistance by force—The latter is our choice.— We have counted the cost of this contest, and find nothing so dreadful as voluntary slavery.—Honor, justice, and humanity forbid us tamely to surrender that freedom which we received from our gallant ancestors, and which our innocent posterity have a right to receive from us. We cannot endure the infamy and guilt of resigning succeeding generations to that wretchedness which inevitably awaits them, if we basely entail hereditary bondage upon them.

OUR cause is juſt. Our union is perfeĉt. Our internal resources are great, and if necessary, foreign assiſtance is undoubtedly attainable.— We gratefully acknowledge, as signal inſtances of the Divine favour toward us, that his Providence would not permit us to be called into this severe controversy, until we were grown up to our present ſtrength, had been previously exercised in war-like operations, and possessed of the means of defending ourselves.—With hearts fortified with these animating refleĉtions, we moſt solemnly, before GOD and the world declare, that, exerting the utmoſt energy of those powers, which our beneficient Creator hath graciously beſtowed upon us, the arms we have been compelled by our enemies to assume, we will, in defiance of every hazard, with unabating firmness and perseverance, employ for the preservation of our liberties, being with one mind resolved, to dye Free-men rather than to live Slaves.

LEST this declaration should disquiet the minds of our friends and fellow subjeĉts in any part of the empire, we assure them, that we mean not to dissolve that Union which has so long and so happily subsiſted between us, and which we sincerely wish to see reſtored.—Necessity has not yet driven us into that desperate measure, or induced us to excite any other nation to war againſt them.—We have not raised armies with ambitious designs of separating from Great-Britain, and eſtablishing independant states.—We fight not for glory or for conquest. We exhibit to mankind the remarkable speĉtacle of a people attacked by unprovoked enemies, without any imputation, or even suspicion, of offence. They boast of their privileges and civilization, and yet proffer no milder conditions than servitude or death.—

IN our own native land, in defence of the freedom that is our birthright, and which we ever enjoyed till the late violation of it—for the proteĉtion of our property, acquired solely by the honeſt induſtry of our fore-fathers and ourselves, againſt violence aĉtually offered, we have taken up arms. We shall lay them down when hoſtilities shall cease on the part of the aggressors, and all danger of their being renewed shall be removed, and not before.

WITH an humble confidence in the mercies of the supreme and impartial Judge and Ruler of the universe, we moſt devoutly implore his divine goodness to conduct us happily through this great conflict, to dispose our adversaries to reconciliation on reasonable terms, and thereby to relieve the empire from the calamities of civil war.

By Order of CONGRESS,

JOHN HANCOCK, PRESIDENT.
Attested,
CHARLES THOMSON, SECRETARY.

PHILADELPHIA, ⎫
JULY 6th, 1775. ⎭

NOTES

1 *JCC,* 2:105–8.

2 Thomas Jefferson, *The Papers of Thomas Jefferson,* ed. Julian P. Boyd, vol. 1 (Princeton: Princeton University Press, 1950), pp. 187–219.

3 Joseph Hewes to James Iredell, July 8, 1775, Duke University Library; to Samuel Johnston, July 8, 1775, Burnett, *Letters,* 1:160. The declaration was printed in the *Pennsylvania Packet* on July 10, 1775, and in the *Pennsylvania Gazette* and *Pennsylvania Journal* on July 12, 1775.

4 *JCC,* 2:171–72.

5 According to John Adams, Penn was aboard ship, prepared to sail, on July 9. The *Pennsylvania Packet,* July 10, reported that his ship, the *Barbados Packet,* had cleared customs. Both the *London Daily Advertiser,* August 15, 1775, and the *London Chronicle,* August 12–15, 1775, reported that he had sailed from Philadelphia on July 12. The former newspaper claimed that he crossed to Bristol in 32 days; the latter set the time at 28 days. For Adams' statement, see his letter to James Warren, July 10, 1775, in *Warren-Adams Letters,* ed. Worthington C. Ford, 2 vols. (1917–25; reprint ed., New York: AMS Press, 1972), 1:79–80. The *London Chronicle,* August 15–17, 1775, carried both the declaration and the address, although the address was continued in its August 17–19, 1775, issue. The *Daily Advertiser* of August 17 carried the declaration.

6 George III, in his speech at the opening of Parliament on November 30, 1774, declared that "a most daring spirit of resistance and disobedience to law still unhappily prevails in the Province of Massachusetts. . . . These proceedings have been countenanced and encouraged in other of my Colonies, and unwarranted attempts have been made to obstruct the Commerce of this Kingdom by unlawful combinations." "You may depend," he continued, "on my firm and steadfast resolution to withstand every attempt to weaken or impair the supreme authority of this Legislature over all the Dominions of my crown. . . ." Force, *American Archives,* 4th ser., 1:1466.

7 The petition to the king, presented on December 21, 1774, through Lord Dartmouth, was laid before Parliament when it reconvened on January 19, 1775. Writing Charles

Thomson on February 5, 1775, Benjamin Franklin related that "it came down among a great Heap of Letters of Intelligence from Governors and officers in America, Newspapers, Pamphlets Handbills, &c., from that Country, the last in the List, and was laid upon the Table with them, undistinguished by any particular Recommendation of it to the Notice of either House." Benjamin Franklin, *The Writings of Benjamin Franklin,* ed. Albert H. Smyth, vol. 6 (New York: Macmillan, 1907), p. 304.

8 For this address, which was presented to the king by the Lords and Commons on February 9, 1775, see Force, *American Archives,* 4th ser., 1:1566.

9 The New England Restraining Act (15 Geo. III, c. 10), which received the royal assent on March 30, 1775, forbade the New England colonies, after July 1, 1775, from trading with any nation but Britain and the British West Indies; after July 20, 1775, it forbade their participation in the North Atlantic fisheries. On April 13 the king approved a second Restraining Act (15 Geo. III, c. 18), laying the same prohibitions on the commerce, but not the fisheries, of Pennsylvania, New Jersey, Maryland, Virginia, and South Carolina. Danby Pickering, ed., *The Statutes at Large . . . ,* vol. 31 (Cambridge, 1775), pp. 4–12, 37–43.

10 Lord North's Conciliatory Proposal, February 20, 1775.

The Twelve United Colonies

by their Delegates in Congress, to the Inhabitants of
Great-Britain

Philadelphia: Printed by
William and Thomas Bradford,
1775

Like their predecessors in the First Continental Congress who had fortified their petition to the king with an address to the people of Great Britain, the members of the Second Congress, having resolved to send another petition to George III, decided to send another address to the British people. On June 3, 1775, a committee, consisting of Richard Henry Lee, Robert R. Livingston, Jr., and Edmund Pendleton, was appointed to prepare the address. The committee brought in a draft on June 27 which was read but not considered again until July 6, when it was debated and recommitted. A fresh draft was reported and debated the next day and, after additional debate on the following day, was approved.[1]

In compiling a bibliography of the official publications of the Continental Congress in 1890, Paul L. Ford stated that Richard Henry Lee "wrote the draft [of the address] which was preserved for a number of years by the family, but has since been lost."[2] *In the Lee Family Papers at Harvard there is a draft of the address in R. H. Lee's hand. It differs markedly from the address adopted on July 8, however, and may be the first draft, which was recommitted on July 6. In the absence of any information about the composition of the address, the exact nature of the Harvard draft must remain conjectural.*

On July 8 Congress ordered the address published and a number of copies sent with Richard Penn, who was sailing for England the next day.[3] *Apparently the Bradfords, with their customary dispatch, published the address in time for Penn to carry it with him. The address was certainly published by July 10, because John Adams sent a copy of it to James Warren on that date.*[4]

FRIENDS, COUNTRYMEN, AND BRETHREN!

BY these, and by every other Appellation that may designate the Ties, which bind *us* to each other, we entreat your serious Attention to this our second Attempt to prevent their Dissolution. Remembrance of former Friendships, Pride in the glorious Achievements of our common Ancestors, and the Affection for the Heirs of their Virtues, have hitherto preserved our mutual Connexion; but when that Friendship is violated by the grossest Injuries; when the Pride of Ancestry becomes our Reproach, and we are no otherwise allied than as Tyrants and Slaves; when reduced to the melancholy Alternative of renouncing your Favour or our Freedom; can we hesitate about the Choice? Let the Spirit of *Britons* determine.

In a former Address we asserted our Rights, and stated the Injuries we had then received. We hoped, that the mention of our Wrongs would have roused that honest Indignation which has slept too long for your Honor, or the Welfare of the Empire. But we have not been permitted to entertain this pleasing expectation. Every Day brought an accumulation of Injuries, and the Invention of the Ministry has been constantly exercised, in adding to the Calamities of your *American* Brethren.

After the most valuable Right of Legislation was infringed; when the Powers assumed by your Parliament, in which we are not represented, and from our local and other Circumstances cannot properly be represented, rendered our Property precarious; after being denied that mode of Trial, to which we have long been indebted for the safety of our Persons, and the preservation of our Liberties; after being in many instances divested of those Laws, which were transmitted to us by our common Ancestors, and subjected to an arbitrary Code, compiled under the auspices of *Roman* Tyrants; after those Charters, which encouraged our Predecessors to brave Death and Danger in every Shape, on unknown Seas, in Deserts unexplored, amidst barbarous and inhospitable Nations, were annulled; when, without the form of Trial, without a public Accusation, whole Colonies were condemned, their Trade destroyed, their Inhabitants impoverished; when Soldiers were encouraged to embrue their Hands in the Blood of *Americans,* by offers of Impunity; when new modes of Trial were instituted for the ruin of the accused, where the charge carried with it the horrors of conviction; when a despotic Government was established in a neighbouring Province, and its Limits extended to every of our Frontiers; we little imagined that any thing could be added to this black Catalogue of unprovoked Injuries; but we have unhappily been deceived, and the late Measures of the *British* Ministry fully convince us, that their object is the reduction of these Colonies to Slavery and Ruin.

To confirm this Assertion, let us recal your attention to the Affairs of *America,* since our last Address. Let us combat the Calumnies of our Enemies; and let us warn you of the dangers that threaten you in our destruction. Many of your Fellow-Subjects, whose situation deprived them of other Support, drew their Maintenance from the Sea; but the deprivation of our Liberty being insufficient to satisfy the resentment of our Enemies, the horrors of Famine were superadded, and a *British* Parliament, who, in better times, were the Protectors of Innocence and the Patrons of Humanity, have, without distinction of Age or Sex, robbed thousands of the Food which they were accustomed to draw from that inexhaustible Source, placed in their neighbourhood by the benevolent Creator.

Another Act of your Legislature shuts our Ports, and prohibits our Trade with any but those States from whom the great Law of self preservation renders it absolutely necessary we should at present withhold our Commerce. But this Act (whatever may have been its design) we consider rather as injurious to your Opulence than our Interest. All our Commerce terminates with you; and the Wealth we procure from other Nations, is soon exchanged for your Superfluities. Our remittances must then cease with our trade; and our refinements with our Affluence. We trust, however, that Laws which deprive us of every Blessing but a Soil that teems with the necessaries of Life, and that Liberty which renders the enjoyment of them secure, will not relax our Vigour in their Defence.

We might here observe on the Cruelty and Inconsistency of those, who, while they publicly Brand us with reproachful and unworthy Epithets, endeavour to deprive us of the means of defence, by their Interposition with foreign Powers, and to deliver us to the lawless Ravages of a merciless Soldiery. But happily we are not without Resources; and though the timid and humiliating Applications of a *British* Ministry should prevail with foreign Nations, yet Industry, prompted by necessity, will not leave us without the necessary Supplies.

We could wish to go no further, and, not to wound the Ear of Humanity, leave untold those rigorous Acts of Oppression, which are daily exercised in the Town of *Boston,* did we not hope, that by disclaiming their Deeds and punishing the Perpetrators, you would shortly vindicate the Honour of the *British* Name, and re-establish the violated Laws of Justice.

That once populous, flourishing and commercial Town is now garrisoned by an Army sent not to protect, but to enslave its Inhabitants. The civil Government is overturned, and a military Despotism erected upon its Ruins. Without Law, without Right, Powers are assumed unknown to the Constitution. Private Property is unjustly invaded. The Inhabitants, daily subjected to the Licentiousness of the Soldiery, are forbid to remove in Defiance of their natural Rights, in Violation of the most solemn Compacts. Or if, after long and wearisome Solicitation, a Pass is procured, their Effects are detained, and even those who are most favoured, have no Alternative but Poverty or Slavery. The Distress of many thousand People, wantonly deprived of the Necessaries of Life, is a Subject, on which we would not wish to enlarge.

Yet, we cannot but observe, that a *British* Fleet (unjustified even by Acts of your Legislature) are daily employed in ruining our Commerce, seizing our Ships, and depriving whole Communities of their daily Bread. Nor will a Regard for your Honour permit us to be silent, while *British* Troops sully your Glory, by Actions, which the most inveterate Enmity will not palliate among civilized Nations, the wanton and unnecessary Destruction of *Charlestown,* a large, ancient, and once populous Town, just before deserted by its Inhabitants, who had fled to avoid the Fury of your Soldiery.

If you still retain those Sentiments of Compassion, by which *Britons* have ever been distinguished, if the Humanity, which tempered the Valour of our common Ancestors, has not degenerated into Cruelty, you will lament the Miseries of their Descendants.

To what are we to attribute this Treatment? If to any secret Principle of the Constitution, let it be mentioned; let us learn, that the Government, we have long revered, is not without its Defects, and that while it gives Freedom to a Part, it necessarily enslaves the Remainder of the Empire. If such a Principle exists, why for Ages has it ceased to operate? Why at this Time is it called into Action? Can no Reason be assigned for this Conduct? Or must it be resolved into the wanton Exercise of arbitrary Power? And shall the Descendants of *Britons* tamely submit to this?—No, Sirs! We never will, while we revere the Memory of our gallant and virtuous Ancestors, we never can surrender those glorious Privileges, for which they fought, bled, and conquered. Admit that your Fleets could destroy our Towns, and ravage our Sea-Coasts; these are inconsiderable Objects, Things of no Moment to Men, whose Bosoms glow with the Ardor of Liberty. We can retire beyond the Reach of your Navy, and, without any sensible Diminution of the Necessaries of Life, enjoy a Luxury, which from that Period you will want—the Luxury of being Free.

We know the Force of your Arms, and was it called forth in the Cause of Justice and your Country, we might dread the Exertion: but will *Britons* fight under the Banners of Tyranny? Will they counteract the Labours, and disgrace the Victories of their Ancestors? Will they forge Chains for their Posterity? If they descend to this unworthy Task, will their Swords retain their Edge, their Arms their accustomed Vigour? *Britons* can never become the Instruments of Oppression, till they lose the Spirit of Freedom, by which alone they are invincible.

Our Enemies charge us with Sedition. In what does it consist? In our Refusal to submit to unwarrantable Acts of Injustce and Cruelty? If so, shew us a Period in your History, in which you have not been equally Seditious.

We are accused of aiming at Independence; but how is this Accusation supported? By the Allegations of your Ministers, not by our Actions. Abused, insulted, and contemned, what Steps have we pursued to obtain Redress? We have carried our dutiful Petitions to the Throne. We have applied to your Justice for Relief. We have retrenched our Luxury, and withheld our Trade.

The Advantages of our Commerce were designed as a Compensation for your Protection: When you ceased to protect, for what were we to compensate?

What has been the Success of our Endeavours? The Clemency of our Sovereign is unhappily diverted; our Petitions are treated with Indignity; our Prayers answered by Insults. Our Application to you remains unnoticed, and leaves us the melancholy Apprehension of your wanting either the Will, or the Power, to assist us.

Even under these Circumstances, what Measures have we taken that betray a Desire of Independence? Have we called in the Aid of those foreign Powers, who are the Rivals of your Grandeur? When your Troops were few and defenceless, did we take Advantage of their Distress and expel them our Towns? Or have we permitted them to fortify, to receive new Aid, and to acquire additional Strength?

Let not *your* Enemies and *ours* persuade you, that in this we were influenced by Fear or any other unworthy Motive. The Lives of *Britons* are ſtill dear to us. They are the Children of our Parents, and an uninterrupted Intercourse of mutual Benefits had knit the Bonds of Friendship. When Hoſtilities were commenced, when on a late Occasion we were wantonly attacked by your Troops, though we repelled their Assaults and returned their Blows, yet we lamented the Wounds they obliged us to give; nor have we yet learned to rejoice at a Victory over *Englishmen.*

As we wish not to colour our Actions, or disguise our Thoughts, we shall, in the simple Language of Truth, avow the Measures we have pursued, the Motives upon which we have acted, and our future Designs.

When our late Petition to the Throne produced no other Effect than fresh Injuries, and Votes of your Legislature, calculated to juſtify every Severity; when your Fleets and your Armies were prepared to wreſt from us our Property, to rob us of our Liberties or our Lives; when the hoſtile Attempts of General *Gage* evinced his Designs, we levied Armies for our Security and Defence. When the Powers veſted in the Governor of *Canada,* gave us Reason to apprehend Danger from that Quarter; and we had frequent Intimations, that a cruel and savage Enemy was to be let loose upon the defenceless Inhabitants of our Frontiers; we took such Measures as Prudence dictated, as Necessity will juſtify. We possessed ourselves of *Crown Point* and *Ticonderoga.* Yet give us leave moſt solemnly to assure you, that we have not yet loſt Sight of the Object we have ever had in View, a Reconciliation with you on conſtitutional Principles, and Reſtoration of that friendly Intercourse, which, to the Advantage of both, we till lately maintained.

The Inhabitants of this Country apply themselves chiefly to Agriculture and Commerce. As their Fashions and Manners are similar to yours, your Markets must afford them the Conveniences and Luxuries, for which they exchange the Produce of their Labours. The Wealth of this extended Continent centres with you; and our Trade is so regulated as to be subservient only to your Intereſt. You are too reasonable to expect, that by Taxes (in Addition to this) we should contribute to your Expence; to believe, after diverting the Fountain, that the Streams can flow with unabated Force.

It has been said, that we refuse to submit to the Reſtrictions on our Commerce. From whence is this Inference drawn? Not from our Words, we have repeatedly declared the Contrary; and we again profess our Submission to the several Acts of Trade and Navigation, passed before the Year 1763, trusting, nevertheless, in the Equity and Justice of Parliament, that such of them as, upon cool and impartial Consideration, shall appear to have imposed unnecessary or grievous Restrictions, will, at some happier Period, be repealed or altered. And we cheerfully consent to the Operation of such Acts of the *British* Parliament, as shall be restrained to the Regulation of our external Commerce, for the Purpose of securing the commercial Advantages of the whole Empire to the Mother Country, and the commercial Benefits of its respective Members; excluding every Idea of Taxation internal or external, for raising a Revenue on the Subjects in *America,* without their Consent.[5]

It is alledged that we contribute nothing to the common Defence. To this we answer, that the Advantages which *Great Britain* receives from the Monopoly of our Trade, far exceed our Proportion of the Expence necessary for that Purpose. But should these Advantages be inadequate thereto, let the Restrictions on our Trade be removed, and we will cheerfully contribute such Proportion when constitutionally required.

It is a fundamental Principle of the *British* Constitution, that every Man should have at least a Representative Share in the Formation of those Laws, by which he is bound. Were it otherwise, the Regulation of our internal Police by a *British* Parliament, who are and ever will be unacquainted with our local Circumstances, must be always inconvenient, and frequently oppressive, working our wrong, without yielding any possible Advantage to you.

A Plan of Accommodation (as it has been absurdly called) has been proposed by your Ministers to our respective Assemblies. Were this Proposal free from every other Objection, but that which arises from the Time of the Offer, it would not be unexceptionable. Can Men deliberate with the Bayonet at their Breast? Can they treat with Freedom, while their Towns are sacked; when daily Instances of Injustice and Oppression disturb the slower Operations of Reason?

If this Proposal is really such as you would offer and we accept, why was it delayed till the Nation was put to useless expence, and we were reduced to our present melancholy Situation? If it holds forth nothing, why was it proposed? Unless indeed to deceive you into a Belief, that we were unwilling to listen to any Terms of Accommodation. But what is submitted to our Consideration? We contend for the Disposal of our Property. We are told that our Demand is unreasonable, that our Assemblies may indeed collect our Money, but that they must at the same Time offer, not what your Exigencies or ours may require, but so much as shall be deemed sufficient to satisfy the Desires of a Minister and enable him to provide for Favourites and Dependants. A Recurrence to your own Treasury will convince you how little of the Money already extorted from us has been applied to the Relief of your Burthens. To suppose that we would thus grasp the Shadow and give up the Substance, is adding Insult to Injuries.

We have nevertheless again presented an humble and dutiful Petition to our Sovereign, and to remove every imputation of Obstinacy, have requested his Majesty to direct some Mode, by which the united Applications of his faithful Colonists may be improved into a happy and permanent Reconciliation. We are willing to treat on such Terms as can alone render an accommodation lasting, and we flatter ourselves that our pacific Endeavours will be attended with a removal of ministerial Troops, and a repeal of those Laws, of the Operation of which we complain, on the one part, and a disbanding of our Army, and a dissolution of our commercial Associations, on the other.

Yet conclude not from this that we propose to surrender our Property into the Hands of your Ministry, or vest your Parliament with a Power which may terminate in our Destruction. The great Bulwarks of our Constitution we have desired to maintain by every temperate, by every peaceable Means; but your Ministers (equal Foes to *British* and *American* freedom) have added to their former Oppressions an Attempt to reduce us by the Sword to a base and abject submission. On the Sword, therefore, we are compelled to rely for Protection. Should Victory declare in your Favour, yet Men trained to Arms from their Infancy, and animated by the Love of Liberty, will afford neither a cheap or easy Conquest. Of this at least we are assured, that our Struggle will be glorious, our Success certain; since even in Death we shall find that Freedom which in Life you forbid us to enjoy.

Let us now ask what Advantages are to attend our Reduction? the Trade of a ruined and desolate Country is always inconsiderable, its Revenue trifling; the Expence of subjecting and retaining it in subjection certain and inevitable. What then remains but the gratification of an ill-judged Pride, or the hope of rendering us subservient to designs on your Liberty.

Soldiers who have sheathed their Swords in the Bowels of their *American* Brethren, will not draw them with more reluctance against you. When too late you may lament the loss of that freedom, which we exhort you, while still in your Power, to preserve.

On the other hand, should you prove unsuccessful; should that Connexion, which we most ardently wish to maintain, be dissolved; should your Ministers exhaust your Treasures and waste the Blood of your Countrymen in vain Attempts on our Liberty; do they not deliver you, weak and defenceless, to your natural Enemies?

Since then your Liberty must be the price of your Victories; your Ruin, of your Defeat: What blind Fatality can urge you to a pursuit destructive of all that Britons hold dear?

If you have no regard to the Connexion that has for Ages subsisted between us; if you have forgot the Wounds we have received fighting by your Side for the extention of the Empire; if our Commerce is not an object below your consideration; if Justice and Humanity have lost their influence on your Hearts; still Motives are not wanting to excite your Indignation at the Measures now pursued; Your Wealth, your Honour, your Liberty are at Stake.

Notwithstanding the Distress to which we are reduced, we sometimes forget our own Afflictions, to anticipate and sympathize in yours. We grieve that rash and inconsiderate Councils should precipitate the destruction of an Empire, which has been the envy and admiration of Ages, and call God to witness! that we would part with our Property, endanger our Lives, and sacrifice every thing but Liberty, to redeem you from ruin.

A Cloud hangs over your Heads and ours; 'ere this reaches you, it may probably burst upon us; let us then (before the remembrance of former Kindness is obliterated) once more repeat those Appellations which are ever grateful in our Ears; let us entreat Heaven to avert our Ruin, and the Destruction that threatens our Friends, Brethren and Countrymen, on the other side of the *Atlantic*.

NOTES

1 *JCC*, 2:79–80, 110, 127, 157, 162.

2 Paul L. Ford, *Some Materials for a Bibliography of the Official Publications of the Continental Congress, 1774–1789* (Boston: Trustees of the Boston Public Library, 1890), p. 7.

3 *JCC*, 2:170. For Penn's departure, see note 5, p. 97.

4 John Adams to James Warren, July 10, 1775, in *Warren-Adams Letters*, ed. Worthington C. Ford, 2 vols. (1917–25; reprint, New York: AMS Press, 1972), pp. 79–80.

5 This sentence repeats verbatim (with the exception of one insignificant phrase) article four of the First Continental Congress' Bill of Rights.

An Address

of the Twelve United Colonies of North-America by
their Representatives in Congress to the People of
Ireland

Philadelphia: Printed by
William and Thomas Bradford,
1775

On March 4, 1775, Arthur Lee wrote to Samuel Adams, recommending that the Congress try to capitalize on the good will of the Irish by amending the nonimportation agreement to exempt them from its force or at least by favoring them with an official explanation of its actions. Congress accepted Lee's advice and on June 3 appointed a committee of four, James Duane, William Livingston, Samuel Adams, and John Adams, to prepare an address to the people of Ireland. Not until July 21 did the committee bring in a draft of the address, which was ordered to lie on the table. On July 28 the address was debated and approved,[1] and soon thereafter the Bradfords published it as a pamphlet. Its first appearance in a newspaper was in the Pennsylvania Packet, *August 7, 1775.*

Friends and Fellow-Subjects!

AS the important contest, into which we have been driven, is now become interesting to every European state, and particularly affects the members of the British Empire, we think it our duty to address you on the subject. We are desirous, as is natural to injured innocence, of possessing the good opinion of the virtuous and humane. We are peculiarly desirous of furnishing *you* with a true state of our motives and objects; the better to enable you to judge of our conduct with accuracy, and determine the merits of the controversy with impartiality and precision.

However incredible it may appear, that, at this enlightned period, the leaders of a nation, which in every age has sacrificed hecatombs of her bravest patriots on the altar of liberty, should presume gravely to assert, and, by force of arms, attempt to establish an arbitrary sway over the lives, liberties, and property of their fellow subjects in America, it is, nevertheless, a most deplorable and indisputable truth.

These colonies have, from the time of their first settlement, for near two centuries, peaceably enjoyed those very rights, of which the Ministry have, for *ten* years past, endeavoured, by fraud and by violence, to deprive them. At the conclusion of the last war, the genius of England and the spirit of wisdom, as if offended at the ungrateful treatment of their sons, withdrew from the British councils, and left that nation a prey to a race of ministers, with whom ancient English honesty and benevolence disdained to dwell. From that period, jealousy, discontent, oppression and discord have raged among all his Majesty's subjects; and filled every part of his dominions with distress and complaint.

Not content with our purchasing of Britain, at her own price, cloathing and a thousand other articles used by near three million of people on this vast Continent; not satisfied with the amazing profits arising from the monopoly of our trade, without giving us either time to breathe after a long, though glorious war, or the least credit for the blood and treasure we have expended in it; Notwithstanding the zeal we had manifested for the service of our Sovereign, and the warmest attachment to the constitution of Britain and the people of England, a black and horrid design was formed, to convert us from freemen into slaves, from subjects into vassals, and from friends into enemies.

Taxes, for the first time since we landed on the American shores, were, without our consent, imposed upon us; an unconstitutional edict to compel us to furnish necessaries for a standing army, that we wished to see disbanded, was issued; and the legislature of New York suspended for refusing to comply with it. Our antient and inestimable right of trial by jury was, in many instances, abolished; and the common law of the land made to give place to Admiralty jurisdictions. Judges were rendered, by the tenure of their commissions, entirely dependent on the will of a Minister. New crimes were arbitrarily created: and new courts, unknown to the constitution, instituted. Wicked and insidious Governors have been set over us; and dutiful petitions, for the removal of even the notoriously infamous Governor *Hutchinson,* were branded with the opprobrious appellation of scandalous and defamatory. Hardy attempts have been made, under colour of parliamentary authority, to seize Americans, and carry them to Great Britain to be tried for offences committed in the Colonies. Ancient charters have no longer remained sacred; that of the Massachusetts Bay was violated; and their form of government essentially mutilated and transformed. On pretence of punishing a violation of some private property, committed by a few disguised individuals, the populous and fluorishing town of Boston was surrounded by fleets and armies; its trade destroyed; its port blocked up; and thirty thousand citizens subjected to all the miseries attending so sudden a convulsion in their commercial metropolis; and, to remove every obstacle to the rigorous execution of this system of oppression, an act of parliament was passed evidently calculated to indemnify those, who might, in the prosecution of it, even embrue their hands in the blood of the inhabitants.

Tho' pressed by such an accumulation of undeserved injuries, America still remembered her duty to her sovereign. A Congress, consisting of Deputies from Twelve United Colonies, assembled. They, in the most respectful terms, laid their grievances at the foot of the throne; and implored his Majesty's interposition in their behalf. They also agreed to suspend all trade with Great Britain, Ireland, and the West Indies; hopeing, by this peaceable mode of opposition, to obtain that justice from the British Ministry which had been so long solicited in vain. And here permit us to assure you, that it was with the utmost reluctance we could prevail upon ourselves, to cease our commercial connexion with your island. *Your* parliament had done us no wrong. *You* had ever been friendly to the rights of mankind; and we acknowledge, with pleasure and gratitude, that *your* nation has produced patriots, who have nobly diſtinguished themselves in the cause of humanity and America. On the other hand, we were not ignorant that the labor and manufactures of Ireland, like those of the silk-worm, were of little moment to herself; but served only to give luxury to those who *neither toil nor spin.* We perceived that if we continued our commerce with you, our agreement not to import from Britain would be *fruitless,* and were, therefore, compelled to adopt a measure, to which nothing but absolute necessity would have reconciled us. It gave us, however, some consolation to reflect, that should it occasion much diſtress, the fertile regions of America would afford you a safe assylum from poverty, and, in time, from oppression also; an assylum, in which many thousands of your countrymen have found hospitality, peace, and affluence, and become united to us by all the ties of consanguinity, mutual intereſt, and affection. Nor did the Congress ſtop here: Flattered by a pleasing expectation, that the juſtice and humanity which had so long characterized the English nation, would, on proper application, afford us relief, they represented their grievances in an affectionate address to their brethren in Britain, and intreated their aid and interposition in behalf of these colonies.

The more fully to evince their respect for their sovereign, the unhappy people of Boſton were requeſted by the Congress to submit with patience to their fate; and all America united in a resolution to abſtain from every species of violence. During this period, that devoted town suffered unspeakably. Its inhabitants were insulted and their property violated. Still relying on the clemency and juſtice of his Majeſty and the nation, they permitted a few regiments to take possession of their town, to surround it with fortifications; and to cut off all intercourse between them and their friends in the country.

With anxious expectation did all America wait the event of their petition. All America laments its fate. Their Prince was deaf to their complaints: And vain were all attempts to impress him with a sense of the sufferings of his American subjects, of the cruelty of their *Task Maſters,* and of the *many Plagues* which impended over his dominions. Inſtead of directions for a candid enquiry into our grievances, insult was added to oppression; and our long forbearance rewarded with the imputation of cowardice. Our trade with foreign ſtates was prohibited; and an act of Parliament passed to prevent our even fishing on our own coaſts. Our peaceable Assemblies, for the purpose of consulting the common safety, were declared seditious; and our asserting the very rights which placed the Crown of Great Britain on the heads of the three successive Princes of the House of Hanover, ſtiled rebellion. Orders were given to reinforce the troops in America. The wild and barbarous savages of the wilderness have been solicited, by gifts, to take up the hatchet againſt us; and inſtigated to deludge our settlements with the blood of innocent and defenceless women and children. The whole country was, moreover, alarmed with the expeċted horrors of domeſtic insurreċtions. Refinements in parental cruelty, at which the genius of Britain must blush! Refinements which admit not of being even recited without horror, or praċtised without infamy! We should be happy, were these dark machinations the mere suggeſtions of suspicion. We are sorry to declare, that we are possessed of the moſt authentic and indubitable evidence of their reality.

The Miniſtry, bent on pulling down the pillars of the conſtitution, endeavoured to ereċt the ſtandard of despotism in America; and if successful, Britain and Ireland may shudder at the consequences!

Three of their moſt experienced Generals are sent to wage war with their fellow-subjeċts: and *America* is amazed to find the name of *Howe* in the catalogue of her enemies: She loved his brother.

Despairing of driving the Coloniſts to resiſtance by any other means than aċtual hoſtility, a detachment of the army at Boſton marched into the country in all the array of war; and, unprovoked, fired upon, and killed several of the inhabitants. The neighbouring farmers suddenly assembled, and repelled the attack. From this, all communication between the town and country was intercepted. The citizens petitioned the General for permission to leave the town, and he promised, on surrendering their arms, to permit them to depart with their other effeċts. They accordingly surrendered their arms, and the General violated his faith. Under various pretences, passports were delayed and denied; and many thousands of the inhabitants are, at this day, confined in the town, in the utmoſt wretchedness and want. The lame, the blind, and the sick, have indeed, been turned out into the neighbouring fields; and some, eluding the vigilance of the centries, have escaped from the town, by swimming to the adjacent shores.

The war having thus began on the part of General Gage's troops, the country armed and embodied. The re-inforcements from Ireland soon after arrived; a vigorous attack was then made upon the provincials. In their march, the troops surrounded the town of Charleſtown, consiſting of about four hundred houses, then recently abandoned to escape the fury of a relentless soldiery. Having plundered the houses, they set fire to the town, and reduced it to ashes. To this wanton waste of property, unknown to civilized nations, they were prompted the better to conceal their approach under cover of the smoak. A shocking mixture of cowardice and cruelty, which then first tarnished the lustre of the British arms, when aimed at a brother's breast! But, blessed be God, they were restrained from committing further ravages, by the loss of a very considerable part of their army, including many of their most experienced officers. The loss of the inhabitants was inconsiderable.

Compelled, therefore, to behold thousands of our Countrymen imprisoned, and men, women and children involved in promiscuous and unmerited misery! When we find all faith at an end, and sacred treaties turned into tricks of state; When we perceive our friends and kinsmen massacred, our habitations plundered, our houses in flames, and their once happy inhabitants fed only by the hand of charity; Who can blame us for endeavouring to restrain the progress of desolation? Who can censure our repelling the attacks of such a barbarous band? Who, in such circumstances, would not obey the great, the universal, the divine law of self-preservation?

Though vilified as wanting spirit, we are determined to behave like men. Though insulted and abused, we wish for reconciliation. Though defamed as seditious, we are ready to obey the laws. And though charged with rebellion, will cheerfully bleed in defence of our Sovereign in a righteous cause. What more can we say? What more can we offer?

But we forbear to trouble you with a tedious detail of the various and fruitless offers and applications we have repeatedly made, not for pensions, for wealth, or for honors, but for the humble boon of being permitted to possess the fruits of honest industry, and to enjoy that degree of Liberty, to which God and the Constitution have given us an undoubted right.

Blessed with an indissoluble union, with a variety of internal resources, and with a firm reliance on the justice of the Supreme Disposer of all human events, we have no doubt of rising superior to all the machinations of evil and abandoned Ministers. We already anticipate the golden period, when liberty, with all the gentle arts of peace and humanity, shall establish her mild dominion in this western world, and erect eternal monuments to the memory of those virtuous patriots and martyrs, who shall have fought and bled and suffered in her cause.

Accept our most grateful acknowledgments for the friendly disposition you have always shewn towards us. We know that *you* are not without your grievances. We sympathize with you in your distress, and are pleased to find that the design of subjugating us, has persuaded administration to dispense to Ireland, some vagrant rays of ministerial sunshine. Even the tender mercies of government have long been cruel towards *you*. In the rich pastures of Ireland, many hungry parricides have fed, and grown strong to labour in its destruction. We hope the patient abiding of the meek may not always be forgotten; and God grant that the iniquitous schemes of extirpating liberty from the British empire may be soon defeated. But we should be wanting to ourselves— we should be perfidious to posterity—we should be unworthy that ancestry from which we derive our descent, should we submit, with folded arms, to military butchery and depredation, to gratify the lordly ambition, or sate the avarice of a British Ministry. In defence of our persons and properties, under actual violation, we have taken up arms; When that violence shall be removed, and hostilities cease on the part of the aggressors, they shall cease on our part also. For the atchievement of this happy event, we confide in the good offices of our fellow-subjects beyond the Atlantic. Of their friendly disposition, we do not yet despond; aware, as they must be, that they have nothing more to expect from the same common enemy, than the humble favour of being last devoured.

By order of the Congress,

JOHN HANCOCK *President*

Philadelphia, July 28. 1775.

NOTES

[1] Pauline Maier, *From Resistance to Revolution* (New York: Alfred A. Knopf, 1972), p. 255; *JCC*, 2:80, 194, 212.

Report on
Lord North's Conciliatory Proposal

Printed from
Dunlap's Pennsylvania Packet,
August 7, 1775

On May 26, 1775, the New Jersey delegates laid before Congress a copy of a resolution introduced in the House of Commons by Lord North on February 20, 1775. North's resolution, commonly called his Conciliatory Proposal, passed the Commons a week later and was sent by Dartmouth on March 3 to the colonial governors for submission to their respective legislatures.[1] Governor William Franklin presented the proposal to the New Jersey Assembly, which resolved on May 20 to submit it to the Congress.[2]

Congress referred the proposal to a committee of the whole, which took no immediate action. On July 22 Congress appointed a committee consisting of Franklin, Jefferson, John Adams, and Richard Henry Lee to report on it.[3] Since Jefferson had written the Virginia House of Burgesses' widely acclaimed answer to the proposal, he was designated the committee's draftsman.[4] On July 25 the committee reported his draft, which was read and ordered to lie on the table. On July 31, it was debated and adopted with minor changes.[5]

The report on North's proposal was first published in the Pennsylvania Packet *on August 7, 1775. Somewhat later, the Bradfords published it as a pamphlet.*

THE several Assemblies of NEW JERSEY, PENNSYLVANIA and VIRGINIA, having refered to the Congress a resolution of the House of Com mons of GREAT BRITAIN, which resolution is in these words, viz.

Lunae, 20° die Feb. 1775.

The House in a Committee on the American papers. Motion made, and question proposed.

THAT *it is the opinion of this Committee, that when the General Council and Assembly, or General Court of any of his Majesty's provinces, or colonies in America, shall propose to make provision, according to the condition, circumstance, or situation of such province, or colony, for contributing their proportion to the common defence (such proportion to be raised under the authority of the General Court, or General Assembly of such province or colony, and disposable by Parliament) and shall engage to make provision also, for the support of the civil government, and the Administration of justice in such province or colony, it will be proper if such proposal shall be approved by his Majesty and the two Houses of Parliament; and for so long as such provision shall be made accordingly, to forbear in respect of such province or colony, to lay any duty, tax, or assessment, or to impose any further duty, tax or assessment, except only such duties as it may be expedient to continue to levy or impose, for the regulation of commerce, the net produce of the duties last mentioned, to be carried to the account of such province or colony respectively.*

The Congress took the said resolution into consideration, and are thereupon of opinion:

That the colonies of America are entitled to the sole and exclusive privilege of giving and granting their own money; that this involves a right of deliberating whether they will make any gift, for what purposes it shall be made, and what shall be it's amount; and that it is a high breach of this privilege for any body of men, extraneous to their constitutions, to prescribe the purposes for which money shall be levied on them, to take to themselves the authority of judging of their conditions, circumstances and situations; and of determining the amount of the contribution to be levied.

That as the colonies possess a right of appropriating their gifts, so are they entitled at all times to enquire into their application, to see that they be not wasted among the venal and corrupt for the purpose of undermining the civil rights of the givers, nor yet be diverted to the support of standing armies, inconsistent with their freedom and subversive of their quiet. To propose therefore, as this resolution does, that the monies given by the colonies shall be subject to the disposal of parliament alone, is to propose that they shall relinquish this right of enquiry, and put it in the power of others to render their gifts, ruinous, in proportion as they are liberal.

That this privilege of giving or of witholding our monies is an important barrier against the undue exertion of prerogative, which if left altogether without controul may be exercised to our great oppression; and all history shews how efficacious is its intercession for redress of grievances and re-establishment of rights, and how improvident it would be to part with so powerful a mediator.

We are of opinion that the proposition contained in this resolution is unreasonable and insidious: unreasonable, because, if we declare we accede to it, we declare without reservation, we will purchase the favour of Parliament, not knowing at the same time at what price they will please to estimate their favor: It is insidious, because, individual colonies, having bid and bidden again, till they find the avidity of the seller too great for all their powers to satisfy; are then to return into opposition, divided from their sister colonies whom the minister will have previously detached by a grant of easier terms, or by an artful procrastination of a definitive answer.

That the suspension of the exercise of their pretended power of taxation being expressly made commensurate with the continuance of our gifts, these must be perpetual to make that so. Whereas no experience has shewn that a gift of perpetual revenue secures a perpetual return of duty or of kind disposition. On the contrary, the Parliament itself, wisely attentive to this observation, are in the established practice of granting their supplies from year to year only.

Desirous and determined as we are to consider in the most dispassionate view every seeming advance towards a reconciliation made by the British Parliament, let our brethren of Britain reflect what would have been the sacrifice to men of free spirits had even fair terms been proffered, as these insidious proposals were with circumstances of insult and defiance. A proposition to give our money, accompanied with large fleets and armies, seems addressed to our fears rather than to our freedom.

With what patience would Britons have received articles of treaty from any power on earth when borne on the point of a bayonet by military plenipotentiaries?

We think the attempt unnecessary to raise upon us by force or by threats our proportional contributions to the common defence, when all know, and themselves acknowledge we have fully contributed, whenever called upon to do so in the character of freemen.

We are of opinion it is not just that the colonies should be required to oblige themselves to other contributions, while Great Britain possesses a monopoly of their trade. This of itself lays them under heavy contribution. To demand therefore, additional aids in the form of a tax, is to demand the double of their equal proportion, if we are to contribute equally with the other parts of the empire, let us equally with them enjoy free commerce with the whole world. But while the restrictions on our trade shut to us the resources of wealth, is it just we should bear all other burthens equally with those to whom every resource is open.

We conceive that the British Parliament has no right to intermeddle with our provisions for the support of civil government, or administration of justice. The provisions we have made are such as please ourselves, and are agreeable to our own circumstances; they answer the substantial purposes of government and of justice, and other purposes than these should not be answered. We do not mean that our people shall be burthened with oppressive taxes to provide sinecures for the idle or the wicked, under colour of providing for a civil list. While Parliament pursue their plan of civil government within their own jurisdiction, we also hope to pursue ours without molestation.

We are of opinion the proposition is altogether unsatisfactory because it imports only a suspension of the mode, not a renunciation of the pretended right to tax us: Because too it does not propose to repeal the several Acts of Parliament passed for the purposes of restraining the trade and altering the form of government of one of our Colonies; extending the boundaries and changing the government of Quebec; enlarging the jurisdiction of the Courts of Admiralty and Vice Admiralty; taking from us the rights of trial by a Jury of the vicinage in cases affecting both life and property; transporting us into other countries to be tried for criminal offences; exempting by mock-trial the murderers of Colonists from punishment; and quartering soldiers on us in times of profound peace. Nor do they renounce the power of suspending our own Legislature, and of legislating for us themselves in all cases whatsoever. On the contrary, to shew they mean no discontinuance of injury, they pass acts, at the very time of holding out this proposition, for restraining the commerce and fisheries of the Provinces of New-England, and for interdicting the trade of other Colonies with all foreign nations and with each other. This proves unequivocally they mean not to relinquish the exercise of indiscriminate legislation over us.

Upon the whole, this proposition seems to have been held up to the world, to deceive it into a belief that there was nothing in dispute between us but the *mode* of levying taxes; and that the Parliament having now been so good as to give up this, the Colonies are unreasonable if not perfectly satisfied: Whereas in truth, our adversaries still claim a right of demanding *ad libitum,* and of taxing us themselves to the full amount of their demand, if we do not comply with it. This leaves us without any thing we can call property. But, what is of more importance, and what in this proposal they keep out of sight, as if no such point was now in contest between us, they claim a right to alter our Charters and established laws, and leave us without any security for our Lives or Liberties. The proposition seems also to have been calculated more particularly to lull into fatal security our well-affected fellow subjects on the other side the water, till time should be given for the operation of those arms, which a British Minister pronounced would instantaneously reduce the "cowardly" sons of America to unreserved submission. But when the world reflects, how inadequate to justice are these vaunted terms; when it attends to the rapid and bold succession of injuries, which, during a course of eleven years, have been aimed at these Colonies; when it reviews the pacific and respectful expostulations, which, during that whole time, were the sole arms we opposed to them; when it observes that our complaints were either not heard at all, or were answered with new and accumulated injury; when it recollects that the Minister himself on an early occasion declared, "that he would never treat with America, till he had brought her to his feet," and that an avowed partisan of Ministry has more lately denounced against us the dreadful sentence *"delenda est Carthago,"* that this was done in presence of a British Senate, and being unreproved by them, must be taken to be their own sentiment, (especially as the purpose has already in part been carried into execution by their treatment of Boston, and burning of Charlestown) when it considers the great armaments with which they have invaded us, and the circumstances of cruelty with which these have commenced and prosecuted hostilities; when these things, we say, are laid together, and attentively considered, can the world be deceived into an opinion that we are unreasonable, or can it hesitate to believe with us, that nothing but our own exertions may defeat the ministerial sentence of death or abject submission.

NOTES

[1] Force, *American Archives*, 4th ser., 2:27-29.

[2] *JCC*, 2:61-63.

[3] Ibid., p. 202.

[4] Thomas Jefferson, *The Papers of Thomas Jefferson*, ed. Julian P. Boyd, vol. 1 (Princeton: Princeton University Press, 1950), p. 170–74.

[5] Ibid., p. 225–33; *JCC*, 2:203, 224.

The Olive Branch Petition

Printed from
Dunlap's Pennsylvania Packet,
Supplement, August 21, 1775

On May 26, 1775, Congress resolved that, in view of the hostilities which the British had begun in Massachusetts, the colonies "be immediately put into a state of defence." But it also resolved "that with a sincere design of contributing by all means in our power . . . to the promotion of this most desireable reconciliation, a humble and dutiful petition be present-ed to his Majesty." On June 3 a committee of five—John Dickinson Thomas Johnson, John Rutledge, John Jay, and Benjamin Franklin—was appointed to prepare a petition to the king.

The committee reported a draft of the petition on June 19.[1] Although it was later claimed that the "subject of the Petition . . . occasioned warm and long debates in Congress,"[2] the Journals *give no details of the contest over it. The petition was considered at length on July 4 and again on July 5, on which date it was approved and ordered to be engrossed.[3] It was signed by the members on July 8 and entrusted to Richard Penn, who sailed for England the next day with instructions to join the colonial agents in presenting it to the king.[4]*

Congress refrained, as it had the preceding fall, from publishing the petition immediately, because, as Thomas Jefferson wrote on July 11, 1775, "a public communication, before it has been presented, may be improper."[5] By the middle of August the members evidently concluded that enough time had elapsed for the petition to reach England and be presented, and they released copies of it to the Philadelphia newspapers. The Pennsylvania Packet *published the petition first in a supplement to its August 21 edition. In the meantime Richard Penn, having reached London, joined Arthur Lee in presenting it at the American Department on the same day.[6] Simultaneous action had also occurred in London and Philadelphia on the October 1774 petition, but in neither case is it possible to determine whether by coincidence or design.*

Lee and Penn presented the petition to Dartmouth personally on September 1, 1775, but since the king on August 23 had issued a proclamation for suppressing rebellion and sedition in the colonies, they could hardly have expected a favorable response. Dartmouth did not disappoint them. "As his Majesty did not receive it on the Throne, no answer would be given," he declared.[7] Rebuffed, Lee and Penn immediately published the petition in the London newspapers with a covering letter, dated

September 4, 1775, attesting its authenticity.[8]

The Olive Branch Petition has always been considered the handiwork of John Dickinson. "Congress gave a signal proof of their indulgence to Mr. Dickinson," Jefferson wrote in his autobiography, "in permitting him to draw their second petition to the King according to his own ideas, and passing it with scarcely any amendment."[9] *Among Dickinson's papers in the R. R. Logan Collection at the Historical Society of Pennsylvania is a draft of a petition to the king dated 1775, in John Jay's hand. Evidently Jay, as a member of the committee to prepare the petition, tried his hand at a draft which, proving unacceptable, was subsequently turned over to Dickinson to use as he could. The Jay draft, which proposes the sending of commissioners to America, resembles the petition as adopted only in its fervent wish for a reconciliation with the mother country.*

<hr />

To the King's Most Excellent Majesty.
Most Gracious Sovereign,

WE your Majesty's faithful subjects of the colonies of New-hampshire, Massachusetts-bay, Rhode island and Providence plantations, Connecticut, New-York, New-Jersey, Pennsylvania, the counties of New Castle, Kent and Sussex on Delaware, Maryland, Virginia, North Carolina and South Carolina, in behalf of ourselves and the inhabitants of these colonies, who have deputed us to represent them in general Congress, entreat your Majesty's gracious attention to this our humble petition.

The union between our Mother Country and these colonies, and the energy of mild and just government, produced benefits so remarkably important, and afforded such an assurance of their permanency and increase, that the wonder and envy of other Nations were excited, while they beheld Great Britain riseing to a power the most extraordinary the world had ever known.

Her rivals observing, that there was no probability of this happy connection being broken by civil dissentions, and apprehending its future effects, if left any longer undisturbed, resolved to prevent her receiving such continual and formidable accessions of wealth and strength, by checking the growth of these settlements from which they were to be derived.

In the prosecution of this attempt events so unfavourable to the design took place, that every friend to the interests of Great Britain and these

127

colonies entertained pleasing and reasonable expectations of seeing an additional force and extention immediately given to the operations of the union hitherto experienced, by an enlargement of the dominions of the Crown, and the removal of ancient and warlike enemies to a greater diſtance.

At the conclusion therefore of the late war, the moſt glorious and advantagious that ever had been carried on by British arms, your loyal coloniſts having contributed to its success, by such repeated and ſtrenuous exertions, as frequently procured them the diſtinguished approbation of your Majeſty, of the late king, and of Parliament, doubted not but that they should be permitted with the reſt of the empire, to share in the blessings of peace and the emoluments of victory and conqueſt. While these recent and honorable acknowledgments of their merits remained on record in the journals and acts of that auguſt legislature the Parliament, undefaced by the imputation or even the suspicion of any offence, they were alarmed by a new syſtem of Statutes and regulations adopted for the adminiſtration of the colonies, that filled their minds with the moſt painful fears and jealousies; and to their inexpressible aſtonishment perceived the dangers of a foreign quarrel quickly succeeded by domeſtic dangers, in their judgment of a more dreadful kind.

Nor were their anxieties alleviated by any tendency in this syſtem to promote the welfare of the Mother Country. For 'tho its effects were more immediately felt by them, yet its influence appeared to be injurious to the commerce and prosperity of Great Britain.

We shall decline the ungrateful task of describing the irksome variety of artifices practised by many of your Majeſtys miniſters, the delusive pretences, fruitless terrors, and unavailing severities, that have from time to time been dealt out by them, in their attempts to execute this impolitic plan, or of traceing thro' a series of years paſt the progress of the unhappy differences between Great Britain and these colonies which have flowed from this fatal source.

Your Majeſtys miniſters persevering in their measures and proceeding to open hoſtilities for enforcing them, have compelled us to arm in our own defence, and have engaged us in a controversy so peculiarly abhorrent to the affection of your ſtill faithful coloniſts, that when we consider whom we must oppose in this contest, and if it continues, what may be the consequences, our own particular misfortunes are accounted by us, only as parts of our diſtress.

Knowing, to what violent resentments and incurable animosities, civil discords are apt to exasperate and inflame the contending parties, we think ourselves required by indispensable obligations to Almighty God, to your Majesty, to our fellow subjects, and to ourselves, immediately to use all the means in our power not incompatible with our safety, for stopping the further effusion of blood, and for averting the impending calamities that threaten the British Empire.

Thus called upon to address your Majesty on affairs of such moment to America, and probably to all your dominions, we are earnestly desirous of performing this office with the utmost deference for your Majesty; and we therefore pray, that your royal magnanimity and benevolence may make the most favourable construction of our expressions on so uncommon an occasion. Could we represent in their full force the sentiments that agitate the minds of us your dutiful subjects, we are persuaded, your Majesty would ascribe any seeming deviation from reverence, in our language, and even in our conduct, not to any reprehensible intention but to the impossibility of reconciling the usual appearances of respect with a just attention to our own preservation against those artful and cruel enemies, who abuse your royal confidence and authority for the purpose of effecting our destruction.

Attached to your Majestys person, family and government with all the devotion that principle and affection can inspire, connected with Great Britain by the strongest ties that can unite societies, and deploring every event that tends in any degree to weaken them, we solemnly assure your Majesty, that we not only most ardently desire the former harmony between her and these colonies may be restored but that a concord may be established between them upon so firm a basis, as to perpetuate its blessings uninterrupted by any future dissentions to succeeding generations in both countries, and to transmit your Majestys name to posterity adorned with that signal and lasting glory that has attended the memory of those illustrious personages, whose virtues and abilities have extricated states from dangerous convulsions, and by securing happiness to others, have erected the most noble and durable monuments to their own fame.

We beg leave further to assure your Majesty that notwithstanding the sufferings of your loyal colonists during the course of the present controversy, our breasts retain too tender a regard for the kingdom from which we derive our origin to request such a reconciliation as might in any manner be inconsistent with her dignity or her welfare. These, related as we are to her, honor and duty, as well as inclination induce us to support and advance; and the apprehensions that now oppress our hearts with unspeakable grief, being once removed, your Majesty will find your faithful subjects on this continent ready and willing at all times, as they ever have been with their lives and fortunes to assert and maintain the rights and interests of your Majesty and of our Mother Country.

We therefore beseech your Majesty, that your royal authority and influence may be graciously interposed to procure us releif from our afflicting fears and jealousies occasioned by the system before mentioned, and to settle peace through every part of your dominions, with all humility submitting to your Majesty's wise consideration, whether it may not be expedient for facilitating those important purposes, that your Majesty be pleased to direct some mode by which the united applications of your faithful colonists to the throne, in pursuance of their common councils, may be improved into a happy and permanent reconciliation; and that in the meantime measures be taken for preventing the further destruction of the lives of your Majesty's subjects; and that such statutes as more immediately distress any of your Majestys colonies be repealed: For by such arrangements as your Majestys wisdom can form for collecting the united sense of your American people, we are convinced, your Majesty would receive such satisfactory proofs of the disposition of the colonists towards their sovereign and the parent state, that the wished for opportunity would soon be restored to them, of evincing the sincerity of their professions by every testimony of devotion becoming the most dutiful subjects and the most affectionate colonists.

That your Majesty may enjoy a long and prosperous reign, and that your descendants may govern your dominions with honor to themselves and happiness to their subjects is our sincere and fervent prayer.

John Hancock

COLONY OF NEW HAMPSHIRE
John Langdon
COLONY OF MASSACHUSETTS-BAY
Thomas Cushing
Saml. Adams
John Adams
Rob. Treat Paine
COLONY OF RHODE-ISLAND AND
PROVIDENCE PLANTATIONS
Step. Hopkins
Sam: Ward
COLONY OF CONNECTICUT
Elipht. Dyer
Roger Sherman
Silas Deane
COLONY OF NEW YORK
Phil. Livingston
Jas. Duane

John Alsop
Frans. Lewis
John Jay
Robt. R. Livingston junr.
Lewis Morris
Wm. Floyd
Henry Wisner
NEW JERSEY
Wil. Livingston
John DeHart
Richd. Smith
PENNSYLVANIA
John Dickinson
B. Franklin
Geo: Ross
James Wilson
Cha. Humphreys
Edwd. Biddle

COUNTIES OF NEW CASTLE
KENT & SUSSEX ON DELAWARE
  Cæsar Rodney
  Tho. M: Kean
  Geo: Read
MARYLAND
  Mat. Tilghman
  Ths. Johnson Junr.
  Wm. Paca
  Samuel Chase
  Thos: Stone
COLONY OF VIRGINIA
  P. Henry Jr.

Richard Henry Lee
Edmund Pendleton
Benja. Harrison
Th: Jefferson
NORTH CAROLINA
Will. Hooper
Joseph Hewes
SOUTH CAROLINA
Henry Middleton
Tho. Lynch
Christ. Gadsden
J. Rutledge
Edward Rutledge

NOTES

[1] *JCC*, 2:65, 79–80, 100.

[2] Burnett, *Letters*, 1:158.

[3] *JCC*, 2:126–27; Silas Deane, Diary, July 4, 1775, Connecticut Historical Society.

[4] For the dates of Penn's departure from Pennsylvania and arrival in England, see note 5, p. 97.

[5] To the President of the Virginia Convention, in Thomas Jefferson, *The Papers of Thomas Jefferson*, ed. Julian P. Boyd, vol. 1 (Princeton: Princeton University Press, 1950), p. 223.

[6] B. D. Bargar, *Lord Dartmouth and the American Revolution* (Columbia, S.C.: University of South Carolina Press, 1965), p. 155.

[7] Penn and Lee to the President of Congress, September 2, 1775, Force, *American Archives*, 4th ser., 3:627.

[8] *London Chronicle*, September 2–5, 1774; *London Daily Advertiser*, September 6, 1775.

[9] Burnett, *Letters*, 1:158.

Address to the Assembly of Jamaica

Printed from
*Journal of the Proceedings of the
Congress Held at Philadelphia, May 10, 1775*
(Philadelphia: Printed by
William and Thomas Bradford, 1775)

Although the First Continental Congress did not communicate officially with Jamaica, the Jamaicans were apprised of its activities through commercial channels. To show that they were not indifferent to a contest over British liberties, the assemblymen of Jamaica, on December 28, 1774, adopted a spirited petition to the king, denying the right of Parliament to tax them without representation and refusing to be "bound by any other laws than such as they themselves had assented to. . . ." [1]

When the petition made its way to the mainland, it was enthusiastically received. The Pennsylvania Gazette *published it on March 1, 1775, and the Bradfords brought it out as a pamphlet.* [2] *The General Assembly of Connecticut passed a resolution thanking the Jamaicans and inviting them to join the struggle by establishing committees of correspondence.* [3]

To acknowledge the support of the Jamaicans, Congress on June 3 appointed a committee consisting of William Hooper, James Wilson, and Thomas Lynch to prepare a letter to the inhabitants of the island. On July 21 the committee reported a draft which was ordered to be laid on the table. The consideration of the address, now directed to the Assembly of Jamaica, was resumed on July 25, on which date it was approved. [4] *The address was not immediately published in the newspapers or, separately, as a pamphlet. Its first public appearance was in December 1775 in the Bradford's printing of the* Journals of Congress.

MR. SPEAKER, AND GENTLEMEN OF THE ASSEMBLY OF JAMAICA,

WE would think ourselves deficient in our duty, if we suffered this Congress to pass over without expressing our esteem for the Assembly of Jamaica.

WHOEVER attends to the conduct of those who have been entrusted with the administration of British affairs, during these last twelve years, will discover in it a deliberate plan to destroy, in every part of the empire, the free constitution, for which Britain has been so long and so justly famed. With a dexterity, artful and wicked, they have varied the modes of attack according to the different characters and circumstances of those whom they meant to reduce. In the East-Indies, where the effeminacy of the inhabitants promised an easy conquest, they thought it unnecessary to veil their tyrannic principles under the thinnest disguise. Without deigning even to pretend a justification of their conduct, they sacrificed the lives of millions to the gratification of their insatiable avarice and lust of power. In Britain, where the maxims of freedom were still known, but where luxury and dissipation had diminished the wonted reverence for them, the attack has been carried on in a more secret and indirect manner: Corruption has been employed to undermine them. The Americans are not enervated by effeminacy, like the inhabitants of India; nor debauched by luxury, like those of Great-Britain: It was therefore judged improper to assail them by bribery, or by undisguised force. Plausible systems were formed; specious pretences were made: All the arts of sophistry were tried to shew, that the British ministry had, by law, a right to enslave us. The first and best maxims of the constitution, venerable to Britons and to Americans, were perverted and prophaned. The power of parliament derived from the people to bind the people, was extended over those from whom it was never derived. It is asserted, that a standing army may be constitutionally kept among us, without our consent. These principles, dishonorable to those who adopted them, and destructive to those, to whom they were applied, were nevertheless carried into execution by the foes of Liberty and of Mankind, acts of parliament, ruinous to America, and unserviceable to Britain, were made to

135

bind us. Armies, maintained by the parliament, were sent over to secure their operation. The power, however, and the cunning of our adversaries, were alike unsuccessful. We refused to their parliaments an obedience, which our judgments disapproved of: We refused to their armies a submission, which spirits, unaccustomed to slavery, could not brook.

BUT while we spurned a disgraceful subjection, we were far from running into rash or seditious measures of opposition. Filled with sentiments of loyalty to our Sovereign, and of affection and respect for our fellow subjects in Britain; we petitioned, we supplicated, we expostulated:—Our prayers were rejected:—Our remonstrances were disregarded:—Our grievances were accumulated. All this did not provoke us to violence.

AN appeal to the justice and humanity of those, who had injured us and were bound to redress our injuries, was ineffectual; we next resolved to make an appeal to their interest; though by doing so we knew we must sacrifice our own, and (which gave us equal uneasiness) that of our friends, who had never offended us, and who were connected with us by a sympathy of feelings under oppressions similar to our own. We resolved to give up our commerce, that we might preserve our liberty. We flattered ourselves, that, when, by withdrawing our commercial intercourse with Britain, which we had an undoubted right either to withdraw or to continue, her trade should be diminished, her revenues impaired and her manufacturers unemployed, our ministerial foes would be induced by interest, or compelled by necessity, to depart from the plan of tyranny which they had so long pursued, and to substitute, in its place, a system more compatible with the freedom of America, and the justice of Britain. That this scheme of non-importation and non-exportation might be productive of the desired effects, we were obliged to include the Islands in it. From this necessity, and from this necessity alone, has our conduct towards them proceeded. By converting your sugar plantations into fields of grain, you can supply yourselves with the necessaries of life: While the present unhappy struggle shall continue, we cannot do more.

BUT why should we make any apology to the patriotic Assembly of Jamaica, who know so well the value of Liberty; who are so sensible of the extreme danger to which ours is exposed; and who foresee how certainly the destruction of ours must be followed by the destruction of their own?

We receive uncommon pleasure from observing the principles of our righteous opposition distinguished by your approbation: We feel the warmest gratitude for your pathetic mediation in our behalf with the crown. It was indeed unavailing—but are you to blame?—Mournful experience tells us, that petitions are often rejected, while the sentiments and conduct of the petitioners entitle what they offer to a happier fate.

That our petitions have been treated with disdain is now become the smallest part of our complaint: Ministerial insolence is lost in ministerial barbarity. It has, by an exertion peculiarly ingenious, procured those very measures, which it laid us under the hard necessity of pursuing, to be stigmatized in parliament as rebellious: It has employed additional fleets and armies for the infamous purpose of compelling us to abandon them: It has plunged us in all the horrors and calamities of civil war: It has caused the treasure and the blood of Britons (formerly shed and expended for far other ends) to be spilt and wasted in the execrable design of spreading slavery over British America: It will not, however, accomplish its aim: In the worst of contingencies, a choice will still be left, which it never can prevent us from making.

The peculiar situation of your Island forbids your assistance. But we have your good wishes.—From the good wishes of the friends of liberty and mankind we shall always derive consolation.

NOTES

[1] Force, *American Archives*, 4th ser., 1:1072–74.

[2] *To the King's Most Excellent Majesty in Council, the Humble Petition and Memorial of the Assembly of Jamaica* (Philadelphia, 1775). Evans, number 14132.

[3] Agnes M. Whitsun, "The Outlook of the Continental American Colonies on the British West Indies," *Political Science Quarterly* 45 (March 1930):84–85.

[4] *JCC*, 2:79–80, 194, 204.

A Speech

to the Six Confederate Nations, Mohawks, Oneidas, Tuscaroras, Onondagas, Cayugas, Senekas, from the Twelve United Colonies, convened in Council at Philadelphia

Printed from
*Journal of the Proceedings of the
Congress Held at Philadelphia, May 10, 1775*
(Philadelphia: Printed by
William and Thomas Bradford, 1775)

On Friday, June 16, 1775, Congress appointed a committee of five—
Philip Schuyler, Patrick Henry, James Duane, James Wilson, and Philip
Livingston—to recommend what steps were "necessary to be taken for
securing and preserving the friendship of the Indian Nations." The
Committee for Indian Affairs, as it was called, brought in its recommen-
dations on June 26. On June 30 the committee was instructed to "prepare
proper talks to the several tribes of Indians, for engaging the continuance
of their friendship to us, and neutrality in our present unhappy disputes
with Great Britain." The committee reported a draft of a speech to the
Six Nations on July 13, one day after Congress had agreed upon a com-
prehensive organization of Indian affairs which created three departments—a northern, middle, and southern—with commissioners in
command in each department. Congress approved the speech on July 13
and ordered that "a similar talk be prepared for the other Indian nations
. . . altering so as to suit the Indians in the several departments." [1] There
is no record, however, of the preparation of other addresses.

On July 18, 1775, President John Hancock sent a copy of the speech
to Schuyler, now commanding American troops in the New York area,
informing him that he, Joseph Hawley, Oliver Wolcott, Turbot Francis,
and Volkert Douw had been appointed commissioners for the Northern
Indian Department. [2] Another copy of the speech was entrusted to
Francis and Douw as they left New York City for Albany on August 7,
1775, to attend a conference with the Six Nations. [3] The conference, which
began on August 25, 1775, with all the commissioners except Hawley
present, concluded on September 1. Congress' speech was read to the
Indians on August 26 and 28. [4] It was first published in the Bradfords'
edition of the Journals of Congress, which appeared during the second
week of December 1775. [5]

BROTHERS, SACHEMS AND WARRIORS,

WE, the Delegates from the Twelve United Provinces, viz.
New-Hampshire, Massachusett's-Bay, Rhode-Island, Connecticut,
New-York, New-Jersey, Pennsylvania, The three Lower Counties of
Newcastle, Kent and Sussex, on Delaware, Maryland, Virginia, North-
Carolina, and South-Carolina, now sitting in General Congress at Phila-
delphia, send this Talk to you our Brothers. We are sixty-five in number,
chosen and appointed by the people throughout all these Provinces and
Colonies, to meet and sit together in one great Council, to consult to-
gether for the common good of the land, and speak and act for them.

BROTHERS, in our consultation we have judged it proper and necessary
to send you this Talk, as we are upon the same island, that you may be
informed of the reasons of this great Council, the situation of our civil
constitution, and our disposition towards you our Indian Brothers *of the
Six Nations and their allies.*

(Three Strings, or a small Belt.)

Brothers and Friends, now attend,

WHEN our fathers crossed the great water and came over to this land,
the King of England gave them a Talk; assuring them that they and
their children should be his children, and that if they would leave their
native country and make settlements, and live here, and buy, and sell,
and trade with their brethren beyond the water, they should still keep
hold of the same covenant chain and enjoy peace—And it was covenant-
ed, that the fields, houses, goods and possessions which our fathers should
acquire, should remain to them as their own, and be their children's
forever, and at their sole disposal.

TRUSTING that this covenant should never be broken, our fathers came
a great distance beyond the great water, laid out their money here, built
houses, cleared fields, raised crops, and through their own labour and

141

industry grew tall and strong.

THEY have bought, sold and traded with England according to agreement, sending to them such things as they wanted, and taking in exchange such things as were wanted here.

THE King of England and his people kept the way open for more than one hundred years, and by our trade became richer, and by a union with us, greater and stronger than the other Kings and people who live beyond the water.

ALL this time they lived in great friendship with us, and we with them; for we are brothers—one blood.

WHENEVER they were struck, we instantly felt as though the blow had been given to us—their enemies were our enemies.

WHENEVER they went to war, we sent our men to stand by their side and fight for them, and our money to help them and make them strong.

THEY thanked us for our love and sent us good Talks, and renewed their promise to be one people forever.

Brothers and Friends, open a kind Ear!

WE will now tell you of the quarrel betwixt the Counsellors of King George and the Inhabitants and Colonies of America.

MANY of his Counsellors are proud and wicked men—They persuade the King to break the covenant chain, and not to send us any more good Talks. A considerable number have prevailed upon him to enter into a new covenant against us, and have torn asunder and cast behind their backs the good old covenant which their ancestors and ours entered into and took strong hold of.

THEY now tell us they will slip their hand into our pocket without asking, as though it were their own; and at their pleasure they will take from us our Charters or written civil Constitution which we love as our lives—also our plantations our houses and goods whenever they please, without asking our leave.—That our vessels may go to *this* Island in the sea, but to *this* or *that* particular Island we shall not trade any more.—

And in case of our non-compliance with these new orders, they shut up our harbours.

BROTHERS, this is our present situation—thus have many of the King's Counsellors and Servants dealt with us.—If we submit, or comply with their demands, you can easily perceive to what State we will be reduced.— If our people labour on the field, they will not know who shall enjoy the crop.—If they hunt in the woods, it will be uncertain who shall taSte of the meat or have the skins.—If they build houses they will not know whether they may sit round the fire, with their wives and children.—They cannot be sure whether they shall be permitted to eat, drink, and wear the fruits of their own labour and induStry.

Brothers and Friends of the Six Nations, attend,

WE upon this Island have often spoke and intreated the King and his Servants the Counsellors, that peace and harmony might Still continue between us—that we cannot part with or loose our hold of the old covenant chain which united our fathers and theirs—that we want to brighten this chain—and keep the way open as our fathers did; that we want to live with them as brothers, labour, trade, travel abroad, eat and drink in peace. We have often asked them to love us and live in such friendship with us as their fathers did with ours.

WE told them again that we judged we were exceedingly injured, that they might as well kill us, as take away our property and the necessaries of life.—We have asked why they treat us thus?—What has become of our repeated addresses and supplications to them? Who hath shut the ears of the King to the cries of his children in America? No soft answer— no pleasant voice from beyond the water has yet sounded in our ears.

BROTHERS, thus Stands the matter betwixt Old England and America. You Indians know how things are proportioned in a family—between the father and the son—the child carries a little pack—England we regard as the father—this Island may be compared to the son.

THE father has a numerous family—both at home and upon this Island. —He appoints a great number of Servants to assiSt him in the government of his family. In process of time, some of his servants grow proud and ill-natured—they were displeased to see the boy so alert and walk on so nimbly with his pack.—They tell the father and advise him to

143

enlarge the child's pack—they prevail—the pack is increased—the child takes it up again—as he thought it might be the father's pleasure—speaks but few words—those very small—for he was loth to offend the father. Those proud and wicked servants finding they had prevailed, laughed to see the boy sweat and ſtagger under his increased load. By and by, they apply to the father to double the boy's pack, because they heard him complain—and without any reason said they—he is a cross child—correct him if he complains any more.—The boy intreats the father—addresses the great servants in a decent manner, that the pack might be lightened—he could not go any farther—humbly asks, if the old fathers, in any of their records, had described such a pack for the child —after all the tears and entreaties of the child—the pack is redoubled— the child ſtands a little, while ſtaggering under the weight—ready to fall every moment.—However he entreats the father once more, though so faint he could only lisp out his laſt humble supplication—waits a while—no voice returns.—The child concludes the father could not hear —those proud servants had intercepted his supplications, or ſtopped the ears of the father.—He therefore gives one ſtruggle and throws off the pack, and says he cannot take it up again—such a weight will crush him down and kill him—and he can but die if he refuses.

UPON this, those servants are very wroth—and tell the father many false ſtories respecting the child—they bring a great cudgle to the father, asking him to take it in his hand and ſtrike the child.

THIS may serve to illuſtrate the present condition of the King's American subjects or children.

AMIDST these oppressions we now and then heard a mollifying and reviving voice from some of the King's wise counsellors, who are our friends and feel for our distresses, when they heard our complaints and our cries, they applied to the King, also told those wicked servants, that this child in America was not a cross boy, it had sufficient reason for crying, and if the cause of its complaint was neglected, it would soon assume the voice of a man, plead for juſtice like a man, and defend its rights and support the old covenant chain of the fathers.

Brothers, liſten!

NOTWITHSTANDING all our intreaties, we have but little hope the King will send us any more good talks, by reason of his evil counsellors; they

144

have persuaded him to send an army of soldiers and many ships of war, to rob and destroy us. They have shut up many of our harbours, seized and taken into possession many of our vessels: The soldiers have struck the blow, killed some of our people, the blood now runs of the American children: They have also burned our houses and towns, and taken much of our goods.

BROTHERS! we are now necessitated to *rise,* and *forced* to fight, or give up our civil constitution, run-away and leave our farms and houses behind us. This must not be. Since the King's wicked counsellors will not open their ears, and consider our just complaints, and the cause of our weeping, and hath given the blow. We are determined to drive away the King's soldiers, and to kill and destroy all those wicked men we find in arms against the peace of the Twelve United Colonies upon this island. We think our cause is just; therefore, hope GOD will be on our side. We do not take up the hatchet and struggle for honor or conquest; but to maintain our civil constitution and religious privileges, the very same for which our forefathers left their native land and came to this country.

Brothers, and Friends!

WE desire you will hear and receive what we have now told you, and that you will open a good ear and listen to what we are now going to say. This is a family quarrel between us and Old England. You Indians are not concerned in it. We don't wish you to take up the hatchet against the King's troops. We desire you to remain at home and not join either side; but keep the hatchet buried deep. In the name and behalf of all our people we ask and desire you to love peace and maintain it, and to love and sympathize with us in our troubles; that the path may be kept open with all our people and yours, to pass and repass, without molestation.

BROTHERS! we live upon the same ground with you. The same Island is our common birth-place. We desire to sit down under the same tree of peace with you: Let us water its roots and cherish its growth, till the large leaves and flourishing branches shall extend to the setting Sun, and reach the skies.

Brothers, observe well!

145

WHAT it is we have asked of you!—Nothing but peace, notwithstanding our present disturbed situation—and if application should be made to you by any of the King's unwise and wicked ministers to join on their side—We only advise you to deliberate with great caution, and in your wisdom look forward to the consequences of a compliance. For if the King's troops take away our property, and destroy us who are of the same blood with themselves—What can you, who are Indians, expect from them afterwards?

THEREFORE we say, Brothers, take care—hold fast to your covenant chain.—You now know our disposition towards you, the Six Nations of Indians and your allies—Let this our good Talk remain at *Onondaga,* your central council house. We depend upon you to send and acquaint your allies to the northward, the seven tribes on the river St. Lawrence, that you have this Talk of ours at the Great Council-Fire of the Six Nations. And when they return, we invite your great men to come and converse farther with us at Albany, where we intend to rekindle the Council-Fire, which your and our ancestors sat round in great friendship.

Brothers and Friends!

We greet you all,

Farewell.

(The large Belt of Intelligence and Declaration.)

Brothers!

WE have said we wish you Indians may continue in peace with one another, and with us the White People. Let us both be cautious in our behaviour towards each other at this critical state of affairs. This Island now trembles, the wind whistles from almost every quarter—let us fortify our minds and shut our ears against false rumours—let us be cautious what we receive for truth, unless spoken by wise and good men. If any thing disagreeable should ever fall out between us, the Twelve United Colonies, and you, the Six Nations, to wound our peace, let us immediately seek measures for healing the breach. From the present situation of our affairs, we judge it wise and expedient to kindle up a small Council-Fire at Albany, where we may hear each others voice, and disclose our minds more fully to one another.

(A small Belt.)

NOTES

1 *JCC*, 2:93, 108, 123, 177–83.

2 Hancock to Schuyler, July 18, 1775, Schuyler Papers, New York Public Library.

3 James Duane to Wolcott, August 7, 1775, Wolcott Papers, Connecticut Historical Society.

4 Force, *American Archives*, 4th ser., 3:477–90.

5 The *Pennsylvania Packet*, December 11, 1775, and *Pennsylvania Journal*, December 13, 1775, announced the Bradfords' edition as "Just Published." James Duane informed his brother on December 9, 1775, that Congress' "proceedings down to the 1st of August are published. . . ." To Cornelius Duane, December 9, 1775, in Southern History Association, *Publications* 7 (1903): 176–77. The *Packet* of December 11, 1775, republished the speech from the *Journals*.

The Letter to the Inhabitants of the Province of Canada

Printed from
U.S. Continental Congress,
Journals of the Continental Congress, 1774–1789,
volume 4, edited by Worthington C. Ford
(Washington: Library of Congress, 1906), p. 85–86[1]

On January 17, 1776, Congress received a letter from Gen. Philip Schuyler officially informing it of the decisive repulse of the American assault on Quebec, December 31, 1775. A committee was appointed on January 18 to consider Schuyler's report and the next day recommended that the army in Canada be reinforced as quickly as possible. On January 23 a committee of three, William Livingston, Thomas Lynch, and James Wilson, was appointed to prepare a letter to the Canadians. The committee reported a draft of the letter on January 24 and Congress immediately approved what became its third letter to the Canadians.[2]

Friends and Countrymen,

OUR former address to you pointed out our rights and grievances, and the means we have in our power, and which we are authorised by the British Conſtitution to use in the maintenance of the former and to obtain a redress of the latter.

We have also shewn you that your liberty, your honor and your happiness are essentially and necessarily connected with the unhappy conteſt, which we have been forced into for the defence of our deareſt privileges.

We see with inexpressible joy the favourable manner in which you have received the juſt and equitable remonſtrances of your friends and countrymen, who have no other views than those of ſtrengthening and eſtablishing the cause of liberty. The services you have already rendered the common cause deserve our acknowledgments, and we feel the juſt obligation your conduct has imposed on us to make our services reciprocal.

The beſt of causes are ſubjeċt to vicissitudes, and disappointments have ever been inevitable. Such is the lot of human nature. But generous souls enlightened and warmed with the sacred fire of liberty become more resolute, as difficulties increase, and surmount with irresiſtible ardor every obſtacle that ſtands between them and the favorite objeċt of their wishes.

We will never abandon you to the unrelenting fury of your and our enemies. Two batallions have already received orders to march to Canada, a part of which are now on their route. Six additional batallions are raising in the United States for the same service and will receive orders to proceed to your province as soon as possible. The whole of these troops will probably arrive in Canada before the miniſterial army under General Carlton can receive any succours. Exclusive of the forces before mentioned, we have direċted that measures be immediately taken to embody two regiments in your country. Your assiſtance in the support and preservation of American liberty affords us the most sensible satisfaċtion and we flatter ourselves that you will seize with zeal and eagerness the favourable moment to co-operate in the success of so glorious an enterprize; and if more considerable forces should become requisite, they shall not fail being sent.

At this period you must be convinced that nothing is so essential to

151

guard our interests and liberty, as efficacious measures to combine our mutual forces, in order that by such an Union of succour and councils, we may be able to baffle the endeavours of an enemy, who, to weaken, may attempt to divide us. To this effect we advise and exhort you to establish associations in your different parishes to the same nature with those, which have proved so salutary to the United Colonies; to elect deputies to form a provincial Assembly, and that said assembly be instructed to appoint delegates to represent them in this Congress. We flatter ourselves with the prospect of the happy moment, when the standard of tyranny shall no longer appear in this land, and we live in full hopes that it will never hereafter find shelter in North America.

Signed in the name and by Order of Congress,

JOHN HANCOCK, *president.*

Philadelphia, January 24, 1776.

NOTES

[1] After adopting this letter, Congress ordered, according to its manuscript journals in the National Archives, "that it be immediately translated." In editing the journals for publication, Ford took the liberty of adding "and printed" to Congress' order. *JCC,* 4:86. The letter does not, however, appear to have been printed in a broadside or in any of the newspapers of the day. Ford printed it from a copy in the papers of Congress.

[2] *JCC,* 4:64–65, 70, 79, 85–86.

Library of Congress Publications for the
Bicentennial of the American Revolution.

The American Revolution: A Selected Reading List. 1968. 38 p. 80 cents. For sale by the Superintendent of Documents, U.S. Government Printing Office, Washington, D.C. 20402.

The American Revolution in Drawings and Prints; a Checklist of 1765–1790 Graphics in the Library of Congress. In press. For sale by the Superintendent of Documents, U.S. Government Printing Office, Washington, D.C. 20402.

The Boston Massacre, 1770, engraved by Paul Revere. Facsim. $2. For sale by the Information Office, Library of Congress, Washington, D.C. 20540.

Creating Independence, 1763–1789: Background Reading for Young People. A Selected Annotated Bibliography. 1972. 62 p. $1.15. For sale by the Superintendent of Documents, U.S. Government Printing Office, Washington, D.C. 20402.

The Development of a Revolutionary Mentality. Papers presented at the first Library of Congress Symposium on the American Revolution. 1972. 158 p. $3.50. For sale by the Information Office, Library of Congress, Washington, D.C. 20540.

English Defenders of American Freedoms, 1774–1778: Six Pamphlets Attacking British Policy. 1972. 231 p. $4.75. For sale by the Superintendent of Documents, U.S. Government Printing Office, Washington, D.C. 20402.

Fundamental Testaments of the American Revolution. Papers presented at the second Library of Congress Symposium on the American Revolution. 1973. 120 p. $3.50. For sale by the Information Office, Library of Congress, Washington, D.C. 20540.

Leadership in the American Revolution. Papers delivered at the third Library of Congress Symposium on the American Revolution. 1974. 135 p. $4.50. For sale by the Information Office, Library of Congress, Washington, D.C. 20540.

Manuscript Sources in the Library of Congress for Research on the American Revolution. 1975. 371 p. $8.70. For sale by the Superintendent of Documents, U.S. Government Printing Office, Washington, D.C. 20402.